W9-BOM-852

Fantastic
After 40!

Pam Farrel

HARVEST HOUSE PUBLISHERS

EUGENE, OREGON

Published in association with the literary agency of Alive Communications, Inc., 7680 Goddard Street, Ste #200, Colorado Springs, CO 80920

Cover photo © Mark Segal / Photographer's Choice / Getty Images

Cover by Left Coast Design, Portland, Oregon

FANTASTIC AFTER 40!

Copyright © 2007 by Pam Farrel
Published by Harvest House Publishers
Eugene, Oregon 97402

Library of Congress Cataloging-in-Publication Data
  Farrel, Pam, 1959-
  Fantastic after 40! / Pam Farrel.
    p. cm.
  ISBN-13: 978-0-7369-1877-0 (pbk.)
  ISBN-10: 0-7369-1877-9
  1. Christian women—Religious life. 2. Aging—Religious aspects—Christianity. 3. Older Christians—Religious life. I. Title. II. Title: Fantastic after forty!
  BV4527.F475 2007
  248.8'43--dc22

2006022911

Printed in the United States of America

07 08 09 10 11 12 13 14 15 / BP-SK / 12 11 10 9 8 7 6 5 4 3 2 1

To my mother, Afton.
Thanks for modeling courage and grace
with every passing year.

⟶

To my loving husband, Bill.
As Robert Browning once said,
"Grow old with me! The best is yet to be."

⟶

To my sweet Seasoned Sisters.
Thanks for all your love, support, and
encouragement. I wouldn't have survived
my forties without each of you.

⟶

To Harvest House,
especially all my over-40 friends there.
Thank you for the vision to encourage,
equip, and inspire women to
finish well and "choose joy."

⟶

To my readers.
My prayer for you is inspired by
my friend Claudia Arp:
"May the rest be the best!"

Contents

The Rest Can Be the Best!

It's not what happens to you.
It's how you take it that counts.

How do you feel about being 40 years old? According to *Time* magazine, there are currently more than 43 million women in America age 40 to 60.[1] We are "baby boomers." We make up the largest age group on the earth today, we are the most affluent consumer group that exists, and we will outlive our male counterparts by an average of 15 years.[2] Girlfriend, we are the majority, we are in the driver's seat, and we have the checkbook!

Yep. There are a few perks I have discovered as a woman who is over 40 today. My 12 favorite fantastic facts are:

1. I can recognize a true friend because she is by my side even when everyone else has left.

2. I have the courage to say no to the vacuum cleaner salesman at my door and the compassion to say yes to Girl Scouts and their Thin Mints. (I mean, with "thin" in the title, they have to be good for you, right?)

3. I know that God will take care of me no matter what the checkbook balance says, what my teen children say, or what my boss or husband may say.

4. I have learned not to sweat the small stuff in life—and that most of life is small stuff. (I am old enough to know

that this phrase is overused—but often that's because we need to remember it. Besides, after 40 we have memory lapses, and that tired old phrase becomes brand-new once again!)

5. I have seen that if you treat people nice, they will usually treat you nice back. And even if they don't, I have lived long enough to see that God works out their "repayment plan" in better ways than I can, so I don't have to even the score.

6. I am not a reflection of choices made by my husband, children, or grandchildren. Even though I lived with the illusion that I could control their choices and actions, I now realize I cannot. I can only control me.

7. I have come to accept that my son can text message from class and still get good grades, and that I usually have to ask him to program the computer, DVD player, clock radio, and iPod. I also realize I really do need to learn these skills because flying him home from college every time I need those things done is getting a little pricey!

8. I can break a nail, run out of gas, lose my car keys, have a fender bender, and get a notice from the IRS, and still not have those things ruin my day.

9. I have seen the day that I want sex even more than my husband.

10. I have accepted that Victoria doesn't have the only secret because a Wal-Mart $3.99 teddy has the same impact as anything from the catalog with anorexic runway models in it.

11. I now like to assume that, for the most part, people mean well even when they don't always decide well.

12. Grace and mercy are things I used to extend to others, but I have come to realize that no one needs them more than I do.

Other Fantastic Facts About Being over 40

- At 40 I learned I could use my "blondness" as an excuse for my forgetfulness and slide right into "menopause" as the reason I can't remember where I parked my car.

- I am not afraid of the "fashion police" if I wear my comfortable shoes rather than heels. I can wear white before Easter and after Labor Day too, if I feel like it.

- I can forget people's names and just call everyone "sweetie," and get away with it.

- I have come to the conclusion that roses, candy, and diamonds don't say "I love you" nearly as well as a 401(k), new tires, or a maid service.

- I get greater joy from the things money cannot buy. Top of the list is when one of my kids calls on the phone to say, "Dear Mom, I am not calling to ask for money. I am calling to tell you thank you." (Don't faint. It really does happen.)

- I have begun to let go of more stress and enjoy life's small pleasures. I rejoice when there is no line at the post office, when a restaurant has my favorite vegetable (asparagus), favorite fruit (strawberries), or key lime pie, when the teen who never picks up his room used his first paycheck to buy me a rose.

- I know when and where the sales are for makeup, clothes, and the all-important undergarment "shapers" with a push-up bra and a tummy flattener. Once I buy it, I realize that I would rather wear my sweats and feel comfortable than that belly-hugging, bottom-lifting, circulation-cutting-off implement designed to never allow you to breathe again.

- Since 40, I feel that memories are better than material goods and people are more precious than pushing my agenda.

- I recognize the real stress relievers: a bubble bath, a solo walk on the beach, the sound of the waves or rain, a warm fire, a cup of tea with honey, and silence—simple silence. ("Can whatever teen has their stereo blaring turn it down so I can savor my silence, please? I am your mother, I have PMS, and I own scissors that can cut the power cord in half! I have the power!")

- If I am tired in the airport, I can lay down on the floor and not care what anyone thinks.

- I can recognize when my teen is trying to manipulate me with the "Mom, you are so beautiful...can I have the car keys?" line. ("Do the dishes, Son, and you might get the keys.")

- I have created hiding places to keep my Dove chocolate out of my kids' mouths. Then realize I don't really want it, so I give it to them anyway.

- I know the shortcuts when the freeway is crowded, the Starbucks with the shortest line, and the cell phone numbers to my lawyer, gynecologist, and massage therapist—and the only one I really want to call is the massage therapist.

Mostly, I have simply learned to laugh more. I recently picked up a birthday card for a friend turning 50, which read:

> *Do the boobs sorta droop and buns sorta sag?*
> *Has the chin multiplied and the eyes kinda bagged?*
> *Do your legs kinda ripple*
> *As you run toward the fridge?*
> *Have your maiden tresses*
> *Turned into drab frizz?*
> *Let's face it, you're labeled,*
> *And there ain't no cure,*
> *But for diplomacy's sake, let's just say you're...*
> *Mature!*[3]

When Reality Sets In

I have always thought that my forties and beyond are *supposed* to be the payoff years. We are supposed to enjoy career success. Our children are supposed to mind beautifully and give us respect and accolades of praise. We are supposed to celebrate years of marital bliss and still be thin and young enough to be mistaken for "trophy wives." At 40 life should be easy as we set the cruise control for peak performance and head for the winner's circle. That's the picture many of us carried in the wallet of our minds as we rounded the track into our forties and on into life's second half.

However, the closer I got to 40, I was observing that, instead of enjoying a life of perfection and ease, the women I knew who were 40 to 65 were struggling with intense issues such as:

- Facing a husband's midlife issues (that sometime led to affairs, divorce, or other forms of family chaos)

- Caring for aging parents

- Raising toddlers if the woman married later or discovered she was unexpectedly pregnant with a "bonus baby blessing"

- Agonizing over teens with raging hormones

Our 40-plus woman is, more often than not, pursuing a career (employment from home, part-time, full-time, owner of a business). She is also running most of the volunteer organizations in the community, from the PTO to youth sports to church ministries. And while she is doing all this, she may be dealing with her own health issues (perimenopause, elevated cholesterol, weight gain, diabetes, breast cancer or other cancers), or her husband might be experiencing health issues (heart attack, high blood pressure, or a need for Viagra).

Meanwhile, many other moms at 40 are dealing with teens and young adult children sowing their wild oats and giving Mom more and more gray hair. Others have teens and young adults who are obedient and grateful but also a significant source of financial stress: paying for high school activities, graduations, college educations, and weddings. Some even have to take on the expenses of their grandchildren because of poor choices by their children. Regard-less of what plates these ladies need to keep spinning, I noticed they are dealing with hot flashes, night sweats, hair growing in places it has never been before, and forgetfulness…(*Where was I going with this? Oh, yes.*) It is no wonder many women feel overweight, over-worked, and overwrought!

The Best Is Yet to Come

You are over 40, but you aren't dead! You are not even on some slippery slope headed to the grave. Seriously, your best accomplish-ments are still ahead. What if the following women had decided they were finished at 40?

Madame Curie created the scientific study of radioactivity, and she was the first woman to be given the Nobel Peace Prize. She is the first, and only, woman to win it twice—the second time at the age of 44.

Condoleezza Rice took the office of National Security Advisor to the president when she was 47.

Jenny Craig began her multimillion-dollar weight loss business after her fortieth birthday, and now millions of women over 40 are grateful.

Renowned artist Grandma Moses didn't even begin painting until she was in her seventies.

Sandra Day O'Conner was still sitting on the Supreme Court when I entered my forties. This first female justice impacted the laws of the land during menopause and beyond.

You can't even be president of the United States until you are 35, and the vast majority of our presidents took office well after their fortieth year of life. (Who's going to run for office, girls?)

You're as Young as You Think

I love the pact that my friends Jack and Robin made in their marriage for the second half of life. The principle behind the agree-ment is great for singles as well as married persons. Here's how Robin describes their decision:

Think young! At my birthday last year I made a pact with my husband to "think young!" I realized that I was already talking myself into being older than I was. You know, saying things like, "Boy, my knees are stiff. I can hardly get up off this chair." Or "I wish the kids would call or visit." Constant talk about cholesterol levels, menopause, blood pressure, and eyesight and hearing loss DO NOT make me an interesting conversation partner. I decided to keep a list of my concerns and keep my annual checkup with my doctor.

I now count on Scripture, such as Psalm 103:5, that tells me God will restore my youth. I wrote "Think young!" next to the name of each month in my day planner, even though I know a day planner isn't young—I really should get a PalmPilot.

My husband and I made a deal. Anytime either one of us made an "old" comment, we would stop, point at the other person, and say loudly enough to be heard, "Think young!"

I Need Some Help Here

I love that attitude. "Think young." But just because I love the attitude doesn't mean I have always had it. As I rounded the corner to my fortieth birthday, my friend Natalie asked me about my melancholy attitude. When I shared that turning 40 was freaking me out a bit, she offered some great advice: "When I turned 50, I decided that life is an attitude, so I decided to name each decade with the goal I wanted to achieve. For example, 'nifty fifty.' "

I pondered her rhyming slogan and thought, *What do I want this decade to represent in my life?* For most of the past six years I had been sitting on the bench watching my three sons excel in sports. Therefore, I decided I needed to get active again. My theme would be, "sporty forty." I celebrated my adventure into my sporty forties with a new tennis outfit, a membership to a health club, and tennis lessons.

As I reflected on Natalie's advice, I realized that many of my friends had been offering words of wisdom. Gayle, Ember, and Pat offered insights on how 18-year-old sons acted when they are trying to fly the nest to gain independence. Debbie counseled me with wise nutritional advice. Marion gave me the latest articles on menopause and other female health-related issues. Marcia gave insights on supplements, and Robin shared her wealth of wisdom on ministering to children as they became adults.

As I crossed the 40 barrier, I realized I needed a support group to handle the oncoming midlife years. When my oldest son began his senior year in high school, I gathered a group of friends and said, "I don't know about you, but I feel like I need some friends around me who want to 'get it' in this season of life." I wanted a circle of friends to whom I didn't have to explain myself because they were also experiencing mood swings, the battle of the bulge, and kids who thought they owned their own lives but lacked the wisdom and resources to pull off independence. I also wanted some trusted mentors—women who were a few steps ahead of me who could help me navigate the release of adult children, the learning curve of becoming a mother-in-law, and the celebration of becoming a grandmother. I wanted to enjoy all these transitions but had no experience to draw from, so I asked my buddies, "Hey, want to do a book study and try to keep a positive attitude as we grow older and handle all that life dishes out to us?"

I received a hearty "amen" from them and the group was birthed. We launched the group by meeting once a month and reading *I'm Too Young to Be This Old!* by Patricia "Poppy" Smith.

We also decided our group needed a name. My teen son saw my friends enter our home one night for our "Christmas Pajama Party" and asked, "So, your crazy ol' lady friends in flannel are coming over?" We definitely didn't like THAT for a name! He would have been grounded for that remark, but I was laughing too hard because it was kind of true.

We were too young for the American Association of Retired

Persons (AARP), so we didn't want any name with the word "senior" in it. Most of us were too old for MOPS (Mothers of Preschoolers), but the word "mature" brought to mind the need to wear sensible shoes, plastic rain bonnets, hairnets, and housecoats, and many of us still felt like red-hot mamas!

We wanted a name that gave us the dignity and respect that was hard to come by at home or in the workplace. We wanted a name that celebrated the fact that we had become "life survivors." We wanted a name that made room for a good sense of humor and a Thighmaster. We noticed that Cher and Sharon Stone could get grown men to salivate when they were close to 50. Madonna could remake herself after a lifetime of wild-side errors. Suzanne Somers and Joan Rivers could dominate QVC, and Liz Taylor had the energy for husbands four and five (or is it six and seven?) We concluded that we could make a dent *for good* in the world in a more substantial, significant way.

I believe, as do my sisters over 40, that we can make a positive impact on the world in the second half of life. We also knew we appreciated and enjoyed the friendships that held our heads above water as the storms of life hit. Those positive relationships were like life preservers tossed into the ocean to rescue those drowning in torrential waves. We needed our sweet sisters to tell us the truth about ourselves, the truth about life, and the truth about God. Together, we could hold on to hope, go forward, and overcome all kinds of life obstacles.

We were sisters. "Seasoned sisters."

And the name stuck. *"Seasoned Sisters"* had a ring to it. We were "seasoned" because, like herbs and seasonings in cooking, our wit, wisdom, experience, talent, and positive outlook made life more palatable and appealing. We noticed we were being used by God to make our corner of the world a bit more appetizing.

Old Is When

1. Going braless pulls all the wrinkles out of your face.

2. Getting lucky means you find your car in the parking lot.

3. An all-nighter means not getting up to use the bathroom.

"Sisters" meant that we cared deeply about one another. We were sisters because we were committed to be there for each other through thick or thin.

The Sisters' Code

As Seasoned Sisters, we felt that growing older meant we needed to set some priorities that would keep us focused on the better half of the second half. Proverbs 31 is a tribute to women, mothers in particular, and there is a precious line in verse 25 that reads "she smiles at the future." We also wanted to smile at the future, so we decided together that:

- We will stay positive no matter how negative life becomes.

- We will keep our sense of humor and laugh at the aging issues as much as possible.

- We will keep an outward focus by serving, giving, and volunteering.

- We will nurture our relationship with God so we can draw on strength that is greater than our own.

- We will take better care of ourselves so we can live longer and stronger.

- We will invest in vital relationships with our spouse (if we have one), our families, and our close friends.

Life Unraveled

It was so kind of God to lead me to begin Seasoned Sisters, because my comfortable world came apart at the seams a couple years into my forties. If my life were described as a hand-crocheted afghan, then one day someone grabbed one piece of yarn and began to unravel my life as I knew it.

Here's just a snapshot of time during what became a transition that lasted more than four years. I was told by my doctor that I was four times more likely to have a heart attack than the average woman because of my family tree. She told me that I needed to make some key life changes or the second half of my life would not be very long.

My husband had been the picture of health, and then suddenly his blood pressure went through the roof. This got our attention because his grandfather died of a stroke at age 47, and his father had a stroke that left him paralyzed and disabled at age 48. Bill was 45. The super-productive husband I had known was going to bed at 6 PM and still seemed exhausted the next day when he rose. His doctors were baffled by his erratic BP that would normalize and then shoot up for no apparent reason.

At that time Bill and I had achieved some measure of success as writers. One of our books had even hit the bestsellers list (*Men Are Like Waffles—Women Are Like Spaghetti*). Bill was also the senior pastor of the largest church in our city, and we were completing a new building project. One day we were traveling and Bill wasn't feeling well, so he went to the doctor. The doctor asked about his life. "Got any stress?" When Bill described his mountain of responsibility, the physician replied, "Bill, you are a people helper. What would you tell someone who came into your office displaying these symptoms?"

Bill replied, "You have some strategic decisions to make and some life change is on the road ahead." *Exactly.* So to make a very long and painful story short, through a series of events and meetings, Bill ended up resigning from the church he had pastored for more than 15 years, a church where we loved the people and they loved us. It was the most difficult, emotionally draining, and painful experience either of us had ever survived. Mixed into the transition were all kinds of friendship and relational issues. The people closest to us fell into two groups: Those who drew closer and offered emotional, spiritual, practical, and financial help, and those who didn't. Some just didn't know what to do, so they stayed away.

Initially, our anxiety level was through the roof. We both would go to bed every night and pray that, when we awoke, we would be freed from this feeling of being dropped down the rabbit hole in *Alice in Wonderland.* We were in a bad dream, and we wanted to wake up where everything was normal again. One of our best friends summarized our experience by saying, "It's like the dots just don't connect." We knew God would make a way for us, but we were looking frantically for the trailhead to get on the new path.

The worry and emotional pain were intense. At times I felt as if I was going to have a heart attack. At night, when I placed my head on my pillow, it felt as though someone were sitting on my chest. Bill and I had taught on midlife transitions (crisis), but now we were experiencing our own.

I was also desperate to do anything to regain my husband's health and somehow protect my own in the process. I was going to bed praying at night that Bill would be alive when I woke up next to him. I took on more of the financial earning responsibility so Bill could recover, rest, and regain his health. We continued to speak and write (and were amazingly successful at it despite all the transitions because God is a good and gracious God). The pace was different than before. For a time, Bill was working half the hours as he previously had, which was still plenty as he had often worked 90 hours per week before he was sick.

While we purposely slowed Bill's pace, I felt my own life stress and responsibility grow. At the time of this life transition, all our sons were teens (at the time 13, 17, and 19). I was trying to keep one kid in college and prepare another for his college education, all during a time when there was a huge income shift. Prior to the health issues, we had poured what savings we had into charitable work, our children's education, and our business expansion. In addition, one company owed us the equivalent of six months of both our salaries. So with about half of the prior cash flow, we were supposed to maintain the same level of responsibilities and obligations. To say the least, the financial pressure was very real on both of us, despite the success we were experiencing in writing and speaking. In addition to our own lives, we had employees, whose families were depending on us at a time when we did not feel very dependable.

One week in particular sticks out to me as a picture of our life. Caleb (then 13) was hit illegally in a football game and had to be rushed to Children's Hospital. We discovered he had internal bleeding and had to have a blood transfusion. He was in ICU for the next eight days. I found myself sitting with Bill next to our son and praying for both their lives to be spared. When we finally brought Caleb home, I had a speaking engagement that the family needed me to keep (because they kind of like groceries in the fridge). I left Caleb in Bill's wonderful care. The first night I was gone, our middle son, Zach, was pulled from his football game with a concussion and knee injury. The next night our oldest, a junior college quarterback, was pulled from the game with what we thought might be a career-ending/scholarship-ending injury. When I landed at the airport, my sister-in-law was on the phone with the news that my 40-year-old brother had experienced a heart attack.

I prayed in desperation, *Lord, who am I supposed to save first?*

One day, while sitting with Caleb in ICU, I picked up a manuscript I was asked to endorse called *Gracepoints: Growth and Guidance During Times of Change* by my friend Jane Rubietta. There is a line in her book that will forever be tattooed onto my heart: "God is working just beyond the headlights of your life."

I am a pretty transparent person, so my feelings show on my face. Even if people didn't know the cause, they could easily pick up that I was experiencing stress. People cared, so they inquired. I just didn't know how to reply when they would ask, "How are you doing?" The answer was either too long, too personal, or too depressing. I didn't want to wreck their day too. Oftentimes when asked, "How are you

Signs of Menopause

1. You sell your home heating system at a yard sale.

2. You have to write Post-it Notes with your kids' names on them.

3. You change your underwear after a sneeze.

---

*Games When
We Are Older*

1. Sag, you're it.

2. Twenty questions shouted into your good ear.

3. Kick the bucket.

4. Red Rover, Red Rover, the nurse says bend over.

5. Musical recliners.

6. Simon says something incoherent.

7. Pin the toupee on the bald guy.

---

doing?" we respond in an Eeyore kind of moan. "Well, pretty good under the circumstances." I love Professor Howard Hendricks' response. "Under the circumstances? What are you doing under there?"

I began to pray and ask God how to answer. God simply responded, "What kind of woman do you want to be, Pam?"

"Lord, I want to be the kind of person who can look at whatever life sends her way and find joy in it. Nehemiah 8:10 says, 'The joy of the LORD is your strength,' and do I ever need strength right now! So joy is the answer."

As a result, I changed my response to the question, "How are you doing?" My new answer became, "Choosin' joy!" (It helped even more when I would say it with a bit of attitude, so I'd fling up my hand up like a cheerleader and shout with a smile, "Choosin' joy!")

And guess what? I found joy! It didn't come all at once, like a tidal wave. It was more like a small spring that began to bubble up. Precious, life-altering, life-saving joy slowly seeped up. Then it bubbled into a geyser of hope and help. Over time it grew bigger and better than Old Faithful in Yellowstone National Park.

Sweet sister, stop reading and try it. Try it right now! Stand up and say out loud, in the closest thing you have to a yell leader voice, "Choosin' joy!" I promise, when you do it, it *will* make you smile. When I give this message at conferences, I ask the audience to say "Choosin' joy!" with California cheerleader attitude. They always laugh and smile when they do it. By choosin' joy, you produce joy!

Joy for the Journey

For some of you, life after 40 will bring challenges much bigger, and pain much deeper, than any I have felt. When you hit those moments, I want you to think about my friend Sheryl. Sheryl was diagnosed with an aggressive form of cancer. She immediately turned to God for help and strength. She meditated on verses like, "My flesh and my heart may fail, but God is the strength of my heart and my portion forever" (Psalm 73:26). Sheryl also gained great encouragement from Dr. David Jeremiah's book *A Bend in the Road* because he too is a cancer survivor. Dr. Jeremiah says, "Disruptive moments are often divine appointments."[4]

Sheryl then began to anticipate how God was going to turn the dark cloud inside out so she could see the silver lining. With that choice, hope pushed its bright ray through the darkness. Sheryl writes this about her chemotherapy:

> We developed our sense of humor to include "tumor humor"—the chemotherapy was cutting edge, only on the market three years and was made of mouse protein. So we developed our own mouse jokes. During the first treatment, I had developed a reaction to the medication. I told the nurse, "I had this unusual craving to build a nest and eat cheese." He said, "I think your tail was trying to grow too fast." I now have all kinds of mouse stuff—my sister-in-law even gave us a pair of Mickey Mouse ears.

Now that is choosin' joy!

'Tis the Season

So *now* how do you feel about being over 40? After 40 used to seem so old to me. I mean, it was those who were over 40 who ran the companies and the community groups, and who seemed to always pay when a family group goes out to dinner. And 50 was celebrated with morbid "over the hill," "one-foot-in-the-grave" birthday cards and black balloon parties. I have never really understood how reminders of impending death can be funny, but I guess if you can laugh at the Grim Reaper, you might just keep him away. Even with all of society's constant reminders of our upcoming mortality, I still think that the after-40 years are the best years of life.

After 40 is the season to remodel your life, remake your future, and renew your passion for the people and priorities you hold dear.

This book is the culmination of the insights I gleaned and the stepping-stones I found to regain joy. But these are not just my ideas or experiences. You will hear the stories of many sisters who have found a way to create a life to look forward to. This book is also a tribute to the incredible faithfulness of our Creator, who takes situations that look like a bunch of discarded scraps and makes a beautiful life quilt from them.

You *can* create a life worth living after 40. Within the chapters of this book are the seeds of hope and the gems of joy that we seasoned sisters can use to create the life we have always dreamed of. Throughout the book, you will see how God turned what was a crisis into a blessing in our life, but more importantly, you will see the steps to take that will help you partner with Him to write a beautiful life plan for your second-half adventure.

Each chapter will include a "Joy Choice" that will help you create a life to look forward to. On the Seasoned Sisters website (www.seasonedsisters.com) are small-group discussion questions for you to dialogue with a friend over lunch or use in your own Seasoned Sisters group. Also on our website you'll find additional helps, such as inspiring verses that will help you "turn up the truth" and give you some hope to hang your heart on. I use verses like this on my weekly prayer walks with my best friends. (Prayer walks are a great idea. You exercise, deepen a friendship, and gain strength for daily life—what can be better than that!)

At the end of this book I am going to ask you, "How are you doing?" And believe me, by then you'll be able to say, "Choosin' joy!"

Joy Choice

I truly believe that we make our choices and our choices make us, so at the end of each chapter I am going to lay out a series of choices that, if you will make them, will help you discover the silver lining in life after 40. Today's joy choice is relatively simple. Practice the positive response whenever anyone asks you during the next week, "How are you?" Your reply will be, "Choosin' joy!"

You Gotta Have Friends

*A friend is like a good bra—hard
to find, supportive, comfortable,
and always close to your heart!*

⌐───⌐

When we built our home, I was out hammering it together with Bill. We were trying to race the stork and complete it before son number three was born. As I was helping Bill frame up walls, I paused and asked, "Honey, why do we have to hammer the 2 x 4s together parallel like this?"

He explained that on bearing walls, and around doors and windows, you hammer the 2 x 4s together so they can carry more weight. Shortly after that, I learned that some contractors call the technique of hammering boards together this way "sistering." Immediately I thought, *What a perfect term for how women strengthen each other in their friendships. We can bear more weight in life if we "sister" one another.*

Midlife is the perfect time to have "sistering" friendships. Midlife is packed with one change, one crisis, one hurdle after another. Over the past few years that our Seasoned Sisters group has existed, we have walked each other through some major life issues:

- Breast cancer and other health issue scares
- The deaths of several parents and caring for many who are aging

- Unwanted divorces
- Business collapse
- Loss of employment or job transition (and many were single moms and sole providers)
- Geographic moves
- Promotions and downsizing
- Reentry into the workforce
- Retirement
- Prodigal children and caring for grandchildren because the prodigal wasn't able
- A husband's depression, and several husbands dealing with medical issues
- Various surgeries of our own or our kids'
- The birth of several "bonus babies" born after mom was 40

In one six-week period, five of us were admitted to the same hospital. A hospital stay became so frequent that one of the members of our friendship circle e-mailed a prayer request. "Pray for me. I just checked in to our favorite spa, otherwise known as Palomar Hospital."

Along with the traumas, in our Seasoned Sisters group we, like most women in midlife, have experienced the revolving doors of change:

- Watching our kids beginning to date—or breaking up
- Helping teens learn to drive—or learn to deal with insurance after wrecking a car
- Sending our children to college—or juvenile hall—or into battle when they join the military
- Rejoicing over an engagement or paying for a wedding— or helping hold a grown child's life together when her spouse abandoned her and her baby

- Attending graduations from middle school, high school, college, or graduate school—or reform school

- Sending some of the kids off on missions trips and honors camps and praying for those who were making decisions that were breaking their mom's hearts and who have become a mission themselves

- Going back to college or back to work—while others retired and bought an RV

- Losing weight, while others found the weight our sisters lost

- Celebrating important wedding anniversaries: 20, 25, 30

- Sitting next to some of our sisters in divorce court

- Mourning the death of spouses

- Attending weddings of our sisters as they gave love another chance

- Welcoming and rejoicing over every grandbaby born, even those who were conceived under less than ideal life choices

- Buoying each other up when our spouses made erratic midlife crisis choices

- Exchanging the latest tips for handling hot flashes, clippings on hormone replacement therapy, and the newest herb remedy for the most annoying menopausal symptom

- Packing each others' houses for a move, trusting she would begin a Seasoned Sisters group in her new location. We welcomed new sisters into the group who moved into our neighborhoods and were brave enough to come hang out with middle-aged women who laugh together, cry together, and hold each other up in the whirlwinds of life.

We've lived through most of the trials and triumphs I will discuss in this book. We survived—no, we *thrived*—because we had each other. Everyone should have friendships like those in our Seasoned Sisters group; women long for friendships such as these. We appreciate the value of friends who are true. In this chapter, you will discover how to be a quality friend. Since *quality attracts quality*, you will make true friends by being a true friend.

Lean on Me

Few things hit a woman closer to the core of her heart than when someone in her family is in crisis. At those times we really need our friends. Betty tells this story of a friend indeed:

> My daughter, Krista, started a healthy diet at the end of her freshman year in high school. Krista weighed only 105 pounds, but she loved sweets and was struggling with complexion problems. She thought she needed to change her eating habits. Because she was on the swim team and worked out three hours a day, I told her eating healthy foods was great, but she needed to consume enough calories to keep her strength up. So, she didn't start the diet until swim season was over. Then Krista started eating healthier foods and eliminated sweets. As the summer wore on, I noticed she was eliminating more and more foods from her diet. Then one Sunday morning after church, I read an article on anorexia that described the personality profile of an anorexic. I knew I was seeing all the signs of the disorder in Krista.
>
> As the summer wore on, Krista continued to lose weight and our family doctor visits weren't helping at all. By September she was down to 89 pounds. Our family vacation at the end of August had been a disaster. Krista didn't want us to go out for meals, and if we did she couldn't find anything on the menu that she would eat. School started, and I was a wreck trying to find help for my daughter.
>
> I went to Holly, the health clerk in our school office. I

knew she was a Christian, and I confided in her. The first thing she said after I told her was, "Betty, we won't stop praying." And from that point on we were both praying all the time. Within days Holly had found out what my insurance covered, whom to call, where to go, what to ask, etc. With her help I finally found a doctor at the UCSD Medical Center who specialized in eating disorders. By the time we met with this doctor at the end of September, Krista's weight was down to 79 pounds. The doctor was very worried about her too, and she told me Krista could easily have heart failure at any time. She set us up with a counselor, and we had weekly visits with the counselor and the doctor for many months.

During those 18 months, Holly's friendship led me into a deeper, stronger relationship with God. I finally came to the point one day, while driving home and praying, that I knew God wanted me to trust Him completely. At this point, my husband, Ken, and I both thought we were going to lose our daughter. I finally gave up and told God that I knew He knew what was best, and I knew Krista wasn't mine, she was His. It was such a hard prayer, but I asked that His will be done, and I told Him I would accept His decision.

As Betty retold the story to me, my eyes filled with tears. To me, this story is even more precious because my son later dated Krista. She was a dear best friend to him. Krista blessed all three of my sons with her kindness and her friendship. The kids both went into a winning season of life, where God honored each one for hanging on tightly to Jesus. Our families rejoiced together when Krista was given the highest honor given at the high school they attended: Knight of the Year.

Sometimes friendship *is* a life-and-death matter.

What Kind of a Friend Does God Want Us to Be?

I feel so privileged to have some incredible friendships. In the period of time I mentioned in chapter 1, when my life felt as though it were unraveling, I saw my friends rise to heights I will never be able to repay. When Caleb was in the hospital, and I was by his side for eight days, my friends rallied. Earlier on the day of his injury, our washing machine broke. Neither Bill nor I had the time to deal with repairing it or working with a repairman. My friends came, divided up the laundry, washed, dried, and folded it. In the process, my friends noticed that I was just like them and had relegated buying for myself to the last thing on the list. They recognized my underwear needed replacing—so they bought me new ones! That is a set of intimate friends.

During that first hard year of turbulent change, friends stood up for our reputation, lobbied leadership on our behalf, gave financially to our nonprofit organization so we could retain employees, brought food and clothes to me at the hospital, sent gifts to Caleb to keep him occupied in his long recovery, and helped me in the office while refusing to take financial remuneration. They walked alongside my husband as he talked through vital career decisions. At the end of that year, they pitched in and threw an amazing twenty-fifth wedding anniversary celebration for us.

Good friends are the safety net under the high wire of life!

Let's Be PALS!

One of my best friends is Lisa Paulsen, the president and founder of You Can! Ministries. Lisa and I give a talk at women's events where we describe what it takes to have a friendship that lasts over the years. We have discovered that pals build their friendships on

P rayer
A ffirmation
L oyalty
S incerity

We have been pals for more than 14 years at the writing of this book.

Pals Pray

I started praying with Lisa the first day I met her. I threw my arms around her because she was experiencing marital discord and desperately wanted God to do a miracle in her marriage. The police had been called to her home numerous times for domestic violence issues. Around Christmas that year, Lisa and her two-year-old found themselves alone. I walked Lisa through the difficult process of restarting a life: courts, counseling for her and her son, navigating single parenting, and the very scary process of beginning to date again. After the divorce, I mentored Lisa in her leadership skills because she had a heart for a ministry to reach out to other single mothers. Lisa was eager to learn, diligent in her counseling, and responsive to mentoring. She grew stronger and wiser at a very rapid pace.

As a part of her restart in life, we developed a support group around her of three trusted friends. They walked her through the hard days of transition and self-examination. When Lisa was feeling stronger emotionally and reentered the social arena, they agreed to check out any man who asked Lisa out. This group also helped her develop a checklist to prequalify men before the first date: Is he a believer? Does he love children? Is he growing spiritually? This could seem drastic to someone who had not come out of an abusive marriage, preceded by a history of "loser" men who had decorated her early dating days. She was willing to do anything this time around to either become a content single mom or meet and marry a wonderful, generous, godly, hardworking man who longed for a family and loved Lisa's son as his own. Amazingly, John was willing to take, and pass, the test, and in 1999 Lisa and John flew Bill and me to Hawaii so Bill could perform the wedding ceremony.

For John's work, Lisa moved to another state, and one day I felt impressed to not just pray for her but to call and pray with her. When I called, I discovered that her pregnancy had become high risk and she had just been taken to the hospital. My prayer support shifted to a long-distance, over-the-phone journey through a very difficult time. Eventually John and Lisa moved back to our area and Lisa and I resumed our face-to-face friendship. Her husband was in job transition, so we prayed. We walked and prayed. We talked and prayed. We prayed for his battle with cancer, and we prayed for a new career path. Eventually God opened up a wonderful job serving in a well-respected church in our area.

Since true friendship is two-sided, Lisa returned the support during my crisis. She walked with me and prayed. She talked with me and prayed. She felt impressed to pray that Bill would be offered a job at the same church at which her husband was employed, even though no positions were available at the time. Eighteen months later, Bill was offered a job at that same church in a position he got to design! It was a perfect fit. Bill was able to minister in the local church the way he loved *and*, as a part of the job, he was given time off for our writing and speaking ministry to enhance marriages and families!

Bill was feeling strong again, his health was in good shape, and this position would help ensure he could maintain his health. When he called to tell me the good news, I was with Lisa and several other of my praying friends (at the time we were actually praying for Bill!). When I told my friends the good news, Lisa (and all the gals) jumped with excitement, squealed with joy, and, of course, prayed in jubilant celebration. After the prayer, Lisa got some chocolate and said, "We need to have a Communion service!"

"With chocolate? Not the usual bread and grape juice?" I asked.

"Chocolate!" Lisa said. "There is something I haven't told you. I have been fasting from chocolate since Bill first got sick and we started praying for his next job assignment. I think we should break my chocolate fast together!"

I was humbled. I knew my chocolate-loving friend had been fasting from her beloved daily Dove experience for more than a year. So we shared Godiva (or maybe it was just Hershey's) together. Lisa and I continue to take prayer walks, and we continue to believe God-sized dreams for each other.

Pals Affirm

Affirming friends can find the positive in any situation. Nicky shares how friends with a "choosin' joy" attitude makes all the difference when life circumstances are not very cooperative:

> My dear friend, Maria, was due to fly out to California from Colorado for a visit. While she was here, we were going to have a jewelry show at my home on Tuesday night. My son, Brent, and daughter, Kayli, were excited for the new carpet transition as well. I had planned my new carpet to be installed the Saturday before Maria was to arrive. On Friday, torrential rain, hail, lightning, and thunder hit. It was one of the biggest storms I had ever seen. So I sent Maria this e-mail:
>
> > Hi, Maria,
> >
> > Well, the rain might delay my carpet installation... YIKES! Everything from the rest of the house is either in my kitchen or garage. A woman with the installers called to make sure there was a dry place to cut the carpet. I said, "Yes, bring it on in and cut it in the house." She said, "No—it has to be someplace outside, like the garage, and out of the rain." In a trembling voice I said, "Everything that used to be in my house is now in my garage. How can my garage possibly be cleared for carpet cutting?" (I think my voice may have jumped a few octaves through this conversation.) She says they would normally cut it in the driveway, but with the huge storm rolling in that's not likely going to be possible. I had to agree with her. I said, "My carpet HAS to be installed tomorrow! (I was becoming a tad frantic.) I have guests coming over Tuesday," to say nothing of the fact that when Lowes called to confirm the installation for tomorrow I told Brent and his friend they could write on the disgusting old carpet with markers. (I hope you're

laughing by now!) I think she started to pick up on my hysteria and kept telling me, "I understand, I understand." I finally told her that no matter what it took, I would clear enough room for them to be able to cut the carpet in my garage. Have the installers come!

I came home from work to find "Greg was here" with footprints traced next to the words and "I've always wanted to do this!" written in huge letters in black indelible marker across my living room carpet. Then in Kayli's room the guys had drawn the outline of a dead body, like in a murder scene! They had included a disgusting brown splat, where I assume the "person" got shot through the heart.

I'm actually laughing as I write this...but it might be hysterical laughter or I'm in some sort of denial.

All will be well, I am certain. You're not nervous about the party now, ARE YOU!?!?!?!?

Is there such a thing as an un-rain dance? My computer will be unplugged in the morning, and I'll be incommunicado through Sunday night. So you'll just have to wait on pins and needles to see if we're going to sit in my beautiful new living room or be sitting Indian-style on disgusting old carpet with dead bodies near by. Paints a nice picture, doesn't it? Happy dreams! :)

Love,

Nicky

⁓

Dear Nicky,

This is one of the funniest things I've ever heard! I don't mean to laugh at your expense, but you do have to admit it is. I laughed out loud right before I read the line you wrote that said "I hope you're laughing by now."

I like the dead body outline the best. We can dress it up with jewelry and no one will notice!

I am not worried at all. It will be lovely to sit in your new living room or very interesting and funny to sit with "the body." Which do you think we would be talking about ten years from now?!

Can't wait to see how it turns out!

Love,

Maria

⌒

Hi, Maria,

I shared my carpet story with Penny, Pam, Robin, and Natalie. Penny wrote back:

Dear Nicky,

I think the carpet sounds fun. Can we bring our own Sharpies? I have lots of cool colors!

Penny

Maria, I'm beginning to hope the carpet doesn't get installed!

Nicky

⌒

Dear Penny,

Good idea! I'll let you all know how things turn out...

I'm beginning to hope the carpet doesn't get installed. Maria thought she could lay out her jewelry on the dead body as part of her demo.

I think we've all gone completely senile!

Hee, hee, hee. Let the laughs begin! See you all Tuesday!

Nicky

Nicky continues, "Thanks to my girlfriends and their amazing ability to see the funny amid the insanity of life (a talent that seems to come in handy way too often of late), I was able to fall asleep with a grin on my face that night before the big install.

"God is so good. After a 3:00 AM torrential rainstorm, God held back the rain until the carpet was delivered. My driveway pond had actually drained dry minutes before the carpet installers arrived, and they were able to cut the new carpet in the driveway by laying it on top of the old carpet they pulled from the house. Not even five minutes after the last piece of new carpet was cut and brought into the house, God let loose the rain from His heavens. My guess is, He was grinning from ear to ear and got a good chuckle out of me freaking out and enjoyed the volley of e-mails we were shooting back and forth. God is very good and has quite a sense of humor. Thank You, Lord, for great friends (and for holding back the rain!)."[1]

Encourage My Heart, Please

Every woman needs a few friends who are encouragers. Life is sometimes so hard and so negative, making it all too easy to spiral downward emotionally unless we hold one another up. I like to think of these kind of friends as fine-tuning friends. Picture good friendships like an electric guitar tuner. Even if I am unable to tune my guitar by ear, a tuner can be attached to tune up the strings so a beautiful melody can be played. In the same way, when we have encouraging friends around us, we can gracefully become a beautiful melody of God's power, love, and plan for hope.

Fine-tuning friends also hold us accountable to live in a way that pleases God. The principle of accountability is found in the Bible everywhere we read the word "exhortation," a term that means "called alongside to bring out the best in another." "Exhortation" is made up of two Greek words, which mean "alongside" and "calling." Exhortation carries the idea of walking alongside someone with compassionate encouragement to help her be her best. "Admonish" is another biblical term that describes the principle of account-ability. It literally means "to put in mind" and carries the idea of putting the right thoughts into the minds of others. So our job as fine-tuning friends is to walk alongside one another, putting the right thoughts into each other's minds in order to help each other reach our God-given potential. That is real *sistering*.

Sistering Saves Lives

Debe is one of those fine-tuning friends in my life. She was the first woman I trained for ministry as a director of women's ministries. Years later I hit a time in life when I was struggling with self-doubt and didn't have any one thing to pin it on. I was feeling like a failure, even though I had just experienced some of my life's greatest successes months before. I had some successful books, I was enjoying traveling for speaking and media, I had a great marriage, my three sons were all doing well, and our women's ministry had just finished a big event that had an incredible impact in our community. But I had put on some weight in my traveling, I was dead-dog tired, and I needed a vacation. At this time someone said something extremely insensitive and hurtful to me, and then a letter four pages long of criticism hit my desk. The final straw came when all my kids and my sweet husband were away doing a camp ministry, and I got a letter in the mail, unsigned, for a weight loss plan and on it was handwritten, "Pam, you really need this!"

Normally I am optimistic, but all the rational, logical evidence for positive success in my life was being clouded over and crowded out by this growing sense of impending failure. Mountains were being made from molehills on every front of my mind. Usually I'd be able to take those things in stride, make changes, and go forward, but severe negative thoughts were plaguing me because of this series of sideswipes. I remember crawling out of bed one night. In tears I sat on the front porch in my nightgown with my arms wrapped around my curled-up knees. I cried out to God, *"Is this what I get? After all I have given, I get picked apart, criticized, and devalued? I'm so tired, God. Why bother? Why try? Why even go on living?"*

The last statement caught my attention. I knew where that came from. "The thief comes only to steal and kill and destroy" (John 10:10). Satan was bombarding my mind with lies from the pit of hell. He wanted to stop me dead in my tracks, if necessary. Since my husband was out of cell range, I called Debe to pray with me. I shared with her what was going on in my life, and as she prayed for me, God gave her a visual impression in her mind of what I was going through. She said to me:

> Pam, I saw you looking into a puddle of water at your reflection. The water was so clear you could see yourself in this liquid mirror. Suddenly, someone threw a rock into the puddle. The water became rippled, and the reflection was distorted. The rock represents the person who has criticized you and hurt you, and the rippled water is how you are seeing yourself as a result. The real Pam, the one God sees, is the same as you saw in the water's reflection before the rock was thrown into the puddle. The real Pam is unharmed. *Only your image has been affected* by the rock, not the real you!

Everyone needs at least one friend like Debe, who tells you the truth so you can keep moving forward in God's clear call. Being sisters who walk alongside one another means we need practical ideas to daily remind one another to think accurate thoughts about ourselves, about God, about life, and about those we love. Below are a few practical ways to tune up others' lives with encouragement.

Twenty-Five Encouraging Ideas

1. When you are thinking of a friend, call her for no other reason then just to say, "I was thinking of you." Leave a prayer on her voice mail, or e-mail her a personalized prayer. For example: *For surely, O Lord , you bless [Lisa, who is] righteous; you surround [her] with your favor as with a shield. May the favor of the Lord our God rest upon [Lisa]; establish the work of [her] hands.*[2]

2. Contribute to her collection as you travel (bring back that

spoon, candle, or figurine). This is especially meaningful if you attach a prayer or a little play on words. For example, attach a note to a spoon from a vacation spot with, "Taste and see that the LORD is good" (Psalm 34:8).

3. Give compliments on her character. It feels great to hear things like, "Thank you for always pointing me back to God." "You are so wise and discerning. I can count on great advice from you." "Your integrity helps me take the high road too."

4. Compliment her clothes, haircut, new shoes—the fun stuff of life too. (It might be on a day her husband forgot to notice, or she might be single, so complimenting her appearance isn't always superficial.)

5. Laugh together. Send funny cards, e-mails, or joke books to lighten her day. The Bible says, "A merry heart does good, like medicine" (Proverbs 17:22 NKJV).

6. Find an activity you enjoy together: gardening, antique shopping, gourmet cooking, scrapbooking. Look for a way to socialize and relax together. Some of the deepest discussions can begin over a pot of soup or flower bed.

7. Work out together. Schedule a gym class or walking date. Nothing says "I love you" like saying, "I love you enough to help you live longer."

8. Buy two of the things you love. I found a purse I loved that you can insert pictures into, so I ordered enough for my closest friends. Bonus points for connecting a new gift to a fantastic old memory you've shared or a brand-new dream you're hoping for.

9. Share a book, a magazine article, or website you found helpful.

10. Give a symbol of your friendship. Was there a special memory or victory you can celebrate? Buy or make something that symbolizes that memory or how you value your friend.

11. Say thanks! Every year around Thanksgiving, I try to give a thank-you gift to the women who have helped carry me forward in God's will that year. One year all of us seemed to be in some state of transition or crisis, so I bought bracelets that were a simple zigzag symbolizing that we pray for one another in the ups and downs of life.

12. Believe in her dream. Believe enough to help her achieve it. Let her teen spend the night with you so she can attend a conference. Send her a care package during finals. Promote her new business to your friendship circle.

13. Stand with her for a breakthrough. One year, a seasoned sister was very concerned about her daughter, and it reminded me of a story author and speaker Jill Briscoe tells of a time that she, too, was fearful and concerned for her daughter. Jill was a speaker at a conference, but she went to the prayer room anyway before the event had begun. She shared her woes and fears with precious older women who were there to pray for the ladies. One of them then said, "I am sure the speaker will say something to encourage you." To which Jill replied, "I am the speaker!" The woman said to Jill that she pictured Jill much like Moses' mother who, to save Moses' life, had to release him by placing him in a basket and letting the basket float down the river. She prayed that God would shut the mouths of the crocodiles in the "river" where Jill had placed her daughter in a basket. Months later Jill received a stuffed alligator in the mail with the mouth tied shut![3] Although Jill's daughter Judy wasn't a prodigal, we moms can worry about many things for our children—even the grown ones. This has become a favorite gift that I give to mothers who are carrying concerns for their teens or young adult children or to moms of prodigals to encourage their hearts.

14. Help her save her marriage by watching her kids, giving her and her spouse a free night in your time-share, or inviting them to a marriage retreat.

15. Give her acceptance, not condemnation, when her kids rebel. And celebrate with her over her children's successes. One of my friends and I each had children who were doing well in high school. We felt excited when they achieved goals that they worked hard on and were recognized by some reward, but we also noticed that others soon tired of the numerous repeated awards our kids won. In response, we found ourselves shutting down and not sharing the exciting praises to God. One day my friend said to me, "Pam, I will always rejoice with you. We are supposed to tell of the goodness of the Lord. So you tell it, girl!" Another friend told the two of us, "I want to know the good things God is doing, even though my daughter is currently a prodigal. Hearing how God is working in other people's kids' lives gives me hope that someday I will see Him work in my daughter's life too." Rejoicing with one another is a precious, rare gift in friendships.

16. Celebrate her achievements. Take her to lunch when she gets a raise.

17. Comfort her in trials. Send cards of encouragement. Send anonymous gifts of cash, gift cards, or coupons if money is tight. We are called to bear one another's burdens.

18. Help her fight temptation. If she fights addictions, have her call you if she is tempted by drugs, alcohol, comfort food, or if she wants to shop or gamble.

19. Forge better life patterns together: Join Weight Watchers or First Place, set a bike or tennis date weekly, take an aerobics class together, or enjoy a heart-smart cooking class.

20. Offer your expertise. My girlfriends have helped me buy a home, learn to use the computer, and redecorate my house. Look around your friendship circle and think, *What do I feel confident in that I could offer a friend?*

21. Help her grow spiritually. Offer to mentor her one-on-one, do a Bible study together or invite her to one you attend, read the same devotional at the same time and meet weekly to discuss what you are learning, share a DVD or a CD of your favorite speakers, pay her way to a conference.

22. Pitch in! If she is painting, toss on your old clothes and help out. If she is moving, help her pack.

23. Come to her aid. If she is pressed to make a deadline at work, bring her family a casserole. If she volunteered to run the PTA fund-raiser and her volunteers bailed, help her out of her jam. Work on a committee beside her and share her assignment.

24. Take pictures of her special days and send them to her by e-mail or create a scrapbook for her.

25. Cheer her on or cheer her up. In Seasoned Sisters, we have an unofficial mascot, a frog. *A frog?* you wonder. Yes, a frog because speaker Daisy Hepburn says FROG stands for:

    F ully

    R ely

    O n

    G od[4]

So we give each other frog socks, frog coasters, frog glasses, frog mugs, frog figurines, and stuffed frogs of all sizes (some of these resources are on the Seasoned Sisters website).

Pals Are Loyal

A wonderful picture of loyal friendship in the Bible is actually a friendship between two guys, but I don't want us to miss the friendship lesson just because the friends are men. The lessons learned are too valuable to get distracted by gender. It is the story of Jonathan and David. In case you need a little background: Saul is king, and Jonathan, his son, is in line to take over the throne at Saul's death. Saul disobeys God, so God says He is taking the throne from Saul (and his family), and then He sends Samuel to select and anoint David as the next king. In those days, if someone contended for the crown, the king or his family adopted mafia mentality and took them out. King Saul was out to kill David, and David was therefore in hiding. But Jonathan was a godly man. Obedience and honoring God were values he held in high esteem. Jonathan was between the proverbial "rock and hard place." Should he be loyal to his dad, who was disloyal to God, or should he be loyal to his friend, who was loyal to God?

David, a leader of legions of soldiers, had the opportunity once to kill Saul, but he held himself back, allowing God and God's timing to rule his destiny. So now, innocent David and his troops are on the run from Saul, but Jonathan manages to track David down. First Samuel 18:3-4 picks up the story: "Then Jonathan made a covenant with David because he loved him as himself. Jonathan stripped himself of the robe that was on him and gave it to David, with his armor, including his sword and his bow and his belt." Jonathan gave David his robe, which denoted Jonathan's identity. Robes of the king and his family were ornate, often purple. In any case, the king and his family were always clothed in a way so that the people *knew* they were royalty. When Jonathan gave David his robe, it was Jonathan's way of saying, "I see you as God's elect. I will follow you."

He gave up the throne in favor of David. Jonathan went so far as to offer David his ongoing friendship, allegiance, loyalty, and support. There is symbolism in the items he handed to David that day. Jonathan gave David his armor, which was a symbol of his new priority to protect David's life over his own. The sword symbolized Jonathan saying, "I will defend you." The bow, an implement of hunting for daily nutritional provisions, symbolized Jonathan saying, "I will look out for your basic needs (food, shelter, etc.)" And with the belt Jonathan indicated, "I will hold you up. If other people malign you, attack you, or seek to harm you, I will not. I will live to hold you in high esteem and will seek to influence others to do the same."

Pals Are Sincere

The apostle Paul explained how he tried to set an example in the way people should treat one another:

> Rather, as servants of God we commend ourselves in every way: in great endurance; in troubles, hardships and distresses; in beatings, imprisonments and riots; in hard work, sleepless nights and hunger; in purity, understanding, patience and kindness; in the Holy Spirit and in sincere love; in truthful speech and in the power of God (2 Corinthians 6:4-7 NIV).

Basically, he was explaining that he suffered hardships so those he loved didn't have to experience such harshness themselves. His readers could trust his sacrifice because it was carried out in purity, understanding, patience, kindness, and sincere love. I love the word "sincere." In the time of the Bible's writing, people used pots and jars made from clay. Before they were sold on the market, they were examined under the sun's light to see if they had any cracks in them. Less expensive pots, those with cracks, had melted wax poured into them to fill the holes and crevices (so they were fakes). But the most pure were marked "sincere" or "without wax." The real deal! Genuine! No imitations!

Isn't that what we all want, friendships that are real? I know I want a friend who will love me when I am successful, beautiful, happy, when my home is gorgeous, when I say insightful, theologically correct things, and my children are well behaved and achieving. But what I want MORE is a friend who will also love me when my children misbehave and act up, when I am grumpy, when I am struggling with my own attitudes and trying to work out the imperfections of my theology, my house is a mess, and I am having a bad hair day—or worse! A real friend hangs in there when we are less than perfect.

True friends are there in life's worst moments. Times when we hear words such as:

- Mom, I'm pregnant.
- I want a divorce.
- I'm having an affair.
- You have cancer.
- Your mother is dying.
- Your dad has Alzheimer's.
- Ma'am, I am sorry, but your son has been in a car accident.
- Honey, I lost my job.
- I'm sorry, but we're downsizing, and your position is being cut.

Fine-tuning friends are also at our side to sister us when we need to hear truth to battle our own fears and discouragements. When we say things such as:

- I want out of this dull, lifeless marriage.
- I don't know what to do with this kid anymore.
- I am so depressed. I don't feel life is worth living.
- I feel so stupid. Why didn't I see the signs?
- I feel like escaping all this stress by jumping off the face of the earth.

Sometimes we need to hear the hard truth to help us snap out of a funk. Several of my friends are determined to help each other "take our thoughts captive" as the Bible encourages (2 Corinthians

10:5) and ask, "What is the truth here?" One friend is so desperate to stop the train when "stinking thinking" runs rampant that she bought a T-shirt that reads "Don't go there!" True friends have seen each other at their worst but stick in there to help each other become their best.

Get Yourselves Some Girlfriends

Lisa, at the end of our "pals" talk, shares a story of our need for girlfriends that are the real "sistering kind." She first read this story to me in her best down-home, Southern mama voice, so as you read it, picture yourself sitting with your best friends on a veranda in the South, drinking sweet tea.

> Young and newly married, I relaxed under a pecan tree on a hot Texas summer day, drinking iced tea and getting to know my new sister-in-law, Estelle. Not much older than I, but already the mother of three, Estelle seemed to me experienced and wise beyond her years.
>
> "Get yourself some girlfriends," she advised, clinking the ice cubes in her glass. "You are going to need girlfriends. Go places with them. Do things with them."
>
> *What a funny piece of advice,* I thought. Hadn't I just gotten married? Hadn't I just joined the couple-world? I was a married woman, for goodness' sake! Not a young girl who needed girlfriends. But just the same I listened to this new sister-in-law. I got myself some girlfriends.
>
> As the years tumbled by, one after another, gradually I came to understand that Estelle knew what she was talking about. I remember that she had said the word "girlfriends" with emphasis. As I went along, I discovered the subtle difference between friends and girlfriends.
>
> You go to work with friends, go to dinner with friends, go to church with friends, and belong to clubs with friends.
>
> You send friends greeting cards. You need friends in

your life. All girlfriends were once only friends. But a girlfriend is different.

I offer this praise of girlfriends. Here is what I know about girlfriends:

Girlfriends don't compete.

Girlfriends bring casseroles and scrub your bathroom when you are sick.

Girlfriends keep your children, and they keep your secrets.

Girlfriends give advice when you ask for it…and sometimes when you don't. Sometimes you take it, sometimes you don't.

Girlfriends don't always tell you that you're right, but they're always honest.

Girlfriends still love you, even when they don't agree with your choices.

Girlfriends might send you a birthday card, but they might not. It does not matter in the least.

Girlfriends laugh with you, and you don't need canned jokes to start the laughter.

Girlfriends pull you out of jams.

Girlfriends don't keep a calendar that lets them know who hosted the last one.

Girlfriends will give a party for your son or daughter when they get married or have a baby, in whichever order that comes.

Girlfriends are there for you, in an instant and truly, when the hard times come.

Girlfriends listen when you lose a job or a husband.

Girlfriends listen when your children break your heart.

Girlfriends listen when your parents' minds and bodies fail.

My girlfriends bless my life. Once we were young, with

no idea of the incredible joys or the incredible sorrows that lay ahead. Nor did we know how much we would need each other.

So, ladies, my advice to you is: "Get yourself some girl-friends."[5]

— Joy Choice —

Call up a girlfriend, or someone you'd like to have for a girl-friend, and do something fun. Friendships begin when one person reaches out; friendships deepen when both women keep reaching out. Do something to encourage your girlfriends this week.

Learning to THRIVE

*I suppose when we wake on January 1 the
world will look the same. But there is a
reminder of the resurrection at the start of
each new year, each new decade. That's why
I like sunrises, Mondays, and new seasons.
God seems to be saying, "With me you can
always have a fresh start."*

At an art exposition, the artist asked the gallery owner whether anyone had been interested in his paintings. The owner said, "I have good news and bad news for you. The good news is that there was a gentleman interested in your paintings, and he asked me whether your work would increase in value after your death, just like that of many other artists. I said, 'Yes, of course, it would. According to your potential, your paintings will increase in value after your death.' So he bought 15 of them. That's the good news." Then the artist asked, "What about the bad news?"

"The guy who bought the paintings is your doctor."

Okay, jokes like that *used* to be funny! But now, over 40, we aren't laughing. Instead, we are asking the question, What makes some people live longer than others? "Monika White, a world-renowned expert on the subject of aging and President of the Center for Healthy Aging, put together a summary on some important similarities among centenarians and factors important to aging well. No definitive findings have resulted from studies of those who live to be 100 years old or older, but similarities have been consistently found, some in health and lifestyle areas *but especially in characteristics and attitudes.* Diet, religion, ethnicity, socioeconomic status, education nor genes (although there is a higher chance of longevity if parents or siblings live a long time), have not accounted for advanced age."[1] Here are some interesting facts:

- Centenarians are not obese.

- Centenarians rarely smoke.

- Centenarians seem to have delayed or avoided age-related health problems such as stroke, heart attacks, cancer, and diabetes, although no one knows why (many Centenarians are donating their bodies to science for study after their deaths).

- Centenarians have a stress-reduction mind-set—they handle stress better than others (sometimes called the "Centenarian Personality").

- Centenarians have a sense of humor—an ability to laugh at themselves and others.

- Centenarians have a sense of hope—they look forward to tomorrow with anticipation.

- Centenarians are engaged—they do something, have an interest, are involved.

- *Centenarians have an ability to cope with loss (and the longer you live, the more you lose—family, including children, friends, sight, hearing, driving, etc.) and still go on with life.*[2]

How we cope when life *doesn't* go our way determines how long we'll make it in the world and the quality of life we will enjoy while here. I reflected on what pulled me through, and what common traits I noticed in the women I admire who have coped well when life dealt them an unfair, unkind, or unwanted hand. I discovered six key factors common among survivors, or "thrivers," as I like to call them. Thrivers have learned how to:

T urn up the truth

H ang their hearts on hope

R eframe the pain

I nhabit praise

V ictory think

E mbrace the future

Turn Up the Truth

When you encounter difficult times, it is easy to let fear control your life. In our book *Men Are Like Waffles—Women Are Liked Spaghetti,* we explain that women "integrate" every aspect of their lives with every other aspect of their lives. In many ways this is quite positive because it means we multitask easily, balance many spinning plates, and maintain many relationships. However, because everything in our life is integrated, one issue touches another and often sets off a domino effect of fear running rampant in our minds. So in a sense, if one thing is wrong in our life—everything is wrong in our life!

Here's a fun sampling of this kind of thinking:

> *Question:* How many women with PMS does it take to screw in a lightbulb?
>
> *Answer:* One. *One!* And do you know *why* it only takes *one?* Because no one else in this house knows *how* to change a lightbulb. They don't even know the bulb is *burned out.* They would sit in this house in the dark for *three days* before they figured it out. And once they figured it out, they wouldn't be able to find the lightbulbs despite the fact that they've been in the *same cupboard* for the past *17 years.* But if they did, by some miracle, find the lightbulbs, *two days later* the chair they dragged from two rooms over to stand on to change the *stupid* lightbulb would *still* be in the *same spot!* And underneath it would be the *crumpled wrapper* the *stupid*

lightbulbs came in. *Why?* Because *no one* in this house *ever* carries out the *garbage!* It's a *wonder* we haven't all *suffocated* from the piles of *garbage* that are *12-feet deep* throughout the *entire house.* The house! *The house!* It would take an *army* to clean this *house...*

Here's a more serious, everyday struggle that threatened to run my emotions into a frenzy as I allowed my "spaghetti fear" to temporarily take over:

Lord, my husband's health is not good. He has been diagnosed with high blood pressure. His dad had a stroke at this age; his grandpa died. Bill is going to die. I can't raise these kids on my own. I can't provide for my family alone. My whole world is Bill, so I wouldn't even want to go on living. God, he is one of the good guys. You promised to take care of the good guys. I thought You were good. Maybe I was wrong. Maybe I have built my whole world on a lie. Maybe You really aren't good, so why serve You? Why read the Bible? Why pray? Why bother doing any of the good stuff? Why even get out of bed? What's the use?

This kind of "stinkin' thinkin'" is straight from the pit of hell. Satan wants you to doubt God's love and character because such doubt will run you straight into despair, depression, distraction, and self-destructive behavior. Then Satan has won. Instead of one issue to deal with, he has spun a web of worry and created multiple, negative issues in your life. That's why the Bible tells us to take "every thought captive" (2 Corinthians 10:5). The original meaning of "to take captive" is the picture of leading worry away and locking it up as a prisoner—away from our minds. Are you worried about something? Picture that worry right now. What is robbing your peace and stealing your joy? Picture yourself walking that worry from the courtroom of your mind into a prison. Now, escort the joy-stealer down the corridor, toss it into solitary confinement, and throw away the key.

I find the easiest way to accomplish this is to tell Satan, "Get out of my life!" I say it out loud and with enthusiasm. I love Romans 16:20 because it declares, "The God of peace will soon crush Satan under your feet." The God of peace has stomping power. In Luke 10:19, Jesus tells His disciples, "Behold, I have given you authority... over all the power of the enemy, and nothing will injure you." When you begin a relationship with Jesus, His Holy Spirit enters your heart and life. All of who Jesus is empowers you. As a result, you can stomp Satan out of your mind and life, if you choose to. When Jesus dealt with Satan in the desert after His baptism, He countered each of Satan's deceptive temptations with God's Word. If it worked for Jesus, it will work for you. James 4:7 makes it clear. "Submit therefore to God. Resist the devil and he *will* flee from you."

God Is Bigger

When life feels overwhelming, as it often can at midlife and beyond, your best emotional lifeboat is a bigger view of God. Betsie Ten Boom once told her sister Corrie, while in a Holocaust concentration camp, "There is no pit so deep that He (God) is not deeper still."[3] My friend Jill Savage, founder of Hearts at Home, says, "Don't look at the mountain. Look at the Mountain Mover." When life is feeling out of control, I ask, What trait of God do I need to better understand? What is my weakness or fear that I can trade in for faith? For example, if I get news that makes me feel that life is spinning out of control, I look up verses on God as the sovereign King who is in complete control. When I am feeling all alone, I look up verses on God as my Father. When I am feeling devalued, neglected, or marginalized, I look up verses on God's love. When I am tempted to react in anger or unkindness, I look up verses on God's patience or kindness.

When life feels unfair or unkind, I need to take action to keep an accurate view of God. God is still the same, no matter how I feel. When I look up verses on God's mercy, goodness, favor, and anointing, I find strength beyond my own ability. The Bible refers to this as "abiding in Christ" in John 15:5-11:

Abide in Me, and I in you...I am the vine, you are the branches; he who abides in Me and I in him, he bears much fruit, for apart from Me you can do nothing...If you abide in Me, and My words abide in you, ask whatever you wish, and it will be done for you. My Father is glorified by this, that you bear much fruit, and so prove to be My disciples. Just as the Father has loved Me, I have also loved you; abide in My love. If you keep My commandments, you will abide in My love; just as I have kept My Father's commandments and abide in His love. These things I have spoken to you so that My joy may be in you, and that your joy may be made full.

The word "abide" means "to dwell or pitch a tent." The goal is to drive in the stakes of your mind and "camp out" on God, His strength, His power, His attributes, and His character. The result of pitching your tent in biblical territory is joy instead of worry. Jesus takes joy in you and your joy is made full.

The power of abiding in Christ is echoed in Isaiah 26:3, "You will keep him in perfect peace, whose mind is stayed on You" (NKJV). The word "stay" means to "lean, lay, rest...lean upon."[4] When I take these verses seriously, I pitch the tent of my life, roll out my sleeping bag, lay down, and rest in the loving, powerful, all-knowing arms of the sovereign Creator, Father God, and Savior of my soul. Author Karen O'Conner, who is in her late sixties and wrote *Getting Old Ain't for Wimps,* advises, "Lean on the Lord—not on a cane—for it is he who has promised, 'Even to your old age and gray hairs, I am he...who will sustain you...' (Isaiah 46:4 NIV)."[5] Lean on God. Camp out with Him with the truth blaring on the stereo of your heart!

Hang Their Hearts on Hope

Hope is necessary when you cannot see what the future holds. You have two choices on how you will navigate through life's second half: fear or faith. I experienced some circumstances I felt were unfair, and I knew that if I focused on the injustice, unkindness, or tough life circumstance, bitterness could lodge in my heart. (We've all been around enough sullen, angry, and bitter women to know we don't want to be that, right?) In my desperation to find hope, I used a daily mantra to forge forward in midlife: *Even when people aren't good, God is good. Even when circumstances aren't good, God is good. Even when I am not good, God is good.*

My friend Teresa Miller once told me, "Pam, I have a choice, bitter or better. I choose to let the pain make me a better person." And she did. Her songs often reverb in my own heart and in concert halls around the world. Bitterness would have robbed the song from her heart. Is a life circumstance robbing your song of joy?

Author Jill Briscoe explains that sometimes we get God and life mixed up. For example, you may have heard someone say (or perhaps you have said), "God, why did You do that?" But when you recount and retrace your steps, you discover it wasn't God who did it. It was either something you did to yourself, some fallout from a broken world, or something Satan engineered. The Bible is pretty clear. "The thief comes only to steal and kill and destroy; I [Jesus] came that they may have life, and have it abundantly" (John 10:10). Check whose fingerprints are on something before you go assigning blame on God.

Does God allow hard things? Sure He does. For example, Jesus' disciples asked about a blind man, "Who sinned, this man or his parents?" "Neither this man nor his parents sinned," said Jesus, "but this happened so that the work of God might be displayed in his life" (John 9:2-3 NIV).

When we read these stories, it seems obvious that God can turn dark into light, but when things look bleak in our life, we sometimes forget that behind all the seemingly miserable or frustrating circumstances sits a powerful, loving, kind, merciful God wanting the *ultimate* best for us and *ultimate* best for His work on earth.

I'm Trading My Sorrow

One day, as I was struggling to hang on to my hope, my friend Tami e-mailed me a verse:

Therefore the Lord [earnestly] waits [expecting, looking, and longing] to be gracious to you; and therefore He lifts Himself up, that He may have mercy on you and show loving-kindness to you. For the Lord is a God of justice. Blessed (happy, fortunate, to be envied) are all those who [earnestly] wait for Him, who expect and look and long for Him [for His victory, for His favor, His love, His peace, His joy, and His matchless, unbroken companionship]!" (Isaiah 30:18 AMP).

I read it. Then I reread it aloud. A paradigm shift occurred in my heart. Any seedlings of bitterness were ripped out as the goodness of God washed over me. Are you still not sure about the goodness of God? Well, neither was I. I was in such a place of emotional pain that I needed to be *fully persuaded* of God's goodness. So, like a good defense attorney obtaining evidence of my client's innocence, I hunted down a host of evidence of God's goodness. Here are a few of the verses I discovered to memorize and meditate on:

I am still confident of this: I will see the goodness of the LORD in the land of the living (Psalm 27:13 NIV).

How great is your goodness, which you have stored up for those who fear you, which you bestow in the sight of men on those who take refuge in you (Psalm 31:19 NIV).

Taste and see that the LORD is good; blessed is the man who takes refuge in him (Psalm 34:8).

For the LORD God is a sun and shield; the LORD bestows favor and honor; no good thing does he withhold from those whose walk is blameless (Psalm 84:11 NIV).

The LORD is good to those whose hope is in him, to the one who seeks him (Lamentations 3:25 NIV).

If you, then, though you are evil, know how to give good gifts to your children, how much more will your Father in heaven give good gifts to those who ask him! (Matthew 7:11 NIV).

Looking back on my life, one of the wisest decisions I made was to get to know God personally. I studied His character, His names, and how He relates to people. God became my best friend. My view of God grew. I learned that He is able to handle anything. Midlife will feel out of control if you lose sight of the good God who is for you (Romans 8:31). I have peace even at midlife because I know God loves me. He has a plan for me that will bring me a future and a hope (Jeremiah 29:11). God is an all-powerful, "Master Chessman," as my friend Natalie so aptly calls Him. He moves the pieces of life around for our good. He is able to work all things together for my good (Romans 8:28).

Let me give you an example. Ever since my sons were little, we'd go on a daily "God hunt." Over dinner, or at bedtime, I'd ask the kids, "Where'd you see the goodness of God today? Where did you see His fingerprints of goodness?"

During the teen years, our God hunt practice became erratic due to the kids' crazy sports schedules and leadership responsibilities. But when Bill got sick and life began to unravel, I resurrected the God hunt. We began to pray and claim the goodness of God. We shared every small scrap of God's goodness with each other. Bill and I began to pray that God's good hand would rest upon our family. Bill did a Bible study of all the places in the Bible where it talks about the good hand of the Lord, or the righteous hand of the Lord. I looked up all the verses on God's goodness, His favor and His anointing. I began to pray those verses over our lives every day.

As I focused on God's goodness, I began to see new areas of imperfection, and fallibility in my own life. So I looked up verses on God's grace, and redemption and prayed His mercy over my humanity. It was agonizing to have to face the negative in me when life itself was so strenuous, but I think it has made me a better leader, a better mother, and a better friend. Looking at myself more accurately motivates me to be a more gracious, giving, and patient person (I hope) because it's hard to be tough on others when I see my own shortcomings.

I now love to pray the mercy of God over my life. I can think of no more wonderful place to be than under His tender care. When Bill and I visited Hawaii, we walked to a beautiful waterfall. Being a swimmer, I swam right out to it and sat under its mighty downpour. It was like a Swedish massage! The water beating down on my shoulders lessened my tension and cooled my overheated body. For me, that's what it feels like to sit under the wonderful waterfall of God's grace, mercy, forgiveness, and loving-kindness! It takes the stress away.

The Boomerang

One day, when I had just received one more hard-to-take phone call packed with even more depressing news, I decided as I hung up the phone to focus on a trait of God. I prayed, "Lord, things feel so out of control, but the truth is that You are in control, You are the sovereign King, so I trust You. Catch my heart and my emotions up to what I know to be true."

The call came in about the time of day that Caleb, my then middle schooler, was getting out of school. I threw on my sunglasses to mask the mascara streaks and tears running down my face before I picked up Caleb. However, he was a pretty perceptive kid, so he asked, "What's wrong, Mom?"

Because I don't believe our kids should be our counselors, I withheld the story and simply said, "It's a grown-up issue, honey. God will take care of it."

"I know, Mom. I am reading this book on the Holy Spirit by Charles Spurgeon, and God is all-knowing, so He knows exactly what you need right now. And God is all-powerful, so He can go get what you need right now. And He is all-loving, so He is motivated to go do what you need right now."

"He already did, Caleb. God sent you! Thank you."

That's what God's goodness will do. As you sow God's truth into your friends' and family's lives, it will boomerang back and bless you.

Reframe the Pain

Bill is known for his unique teaching from the book of James: "Consider it all joy, my brethren, when you encounter various trials, knowing that the testing of your faith produces endurance. And let endurance have its perfect result, so that you may be perfect and complete, lacking in nothing" (James 1:2-4). This part is familiar to many. But the question begs to be asked, "How? How can I consider it all joy?" Verse 5, the very next verse, answers the question: "But if any of you lacks wisdom, let him ask of God, who gives to all generously and without reproach, and it will be given to him." Bill encourages, "When you want to ask 'Why?' instead ask for wisdom."

When we ask for wisdom, wisdom to know God better, wisdom for the next step on the journey, wisdom to know what to do, the verse says God will give it. He gives it without reproach, meaning He won't mock us for asking or belittle our spirituality for asking. He will never say, "Come on. You should know this by now!" Nope. That is not in His nature. Compassion is. Verse 5 also says God gives wisdom "generously," like a rich cake piled high with luscious sweet frosting. When we quit asking Why? Why me? Why now? Why this? and instead ask for wisdom, God reframes the pain and we can move into the Promised Land of hope where He transforms our painful situations into something worthwhile.

Musician Connie Kennemer did just this when the unthinkable happened to her. Connie's grown son, struggling with a bipolar disorder, committed suicide. To navigate the path of pain, God helped Connie reframe the experience. She shares how her friends helped her see Todd's journey differently. The voices of her friends replayed truth to her heart. Connie sent me the following e-mail:

> The first "voice" belongs to Barbara, my prayer partner at my church. Three evenings after Todd's death, we had a memorial service. As Rex and I gathered there with 60-plus of Todd's friends (and our friends), a gathering was taking place at my church back home to pray for us and

reflect on Todd's life. Barb wrote her remembrances of the evening: "As our prayer time ended, we listened to Connie's prophetic song—'Fly Away'—that starts with young Todd's lilting voice singing, 'He's still working on me.' My heart soars to know that God is NOT still working on Todd. His work is complete. I heard Connie's voice. 'Todd has flown away, into the very arms of Jesus.'"

Barb's reflections resonated with another voice—Mary Jane, the leader of my Moms in Touch prayer group. She reminded me of the attribute we had used to praise the Lord the day of Todd's death—God Is Our Deliverer. "Connie, God *answered our prayer for Todd!* The Lord delivered him!" Only those who loved Todd so well and prayed for him for so long could say that. My spirit affirmed her testimony, her witness.

Then there is Margaret. I am going to read the letter she wrote me. "Dear Connie—I'm not sure why, but I think I am supposed to tell you about the experience I had at church last Sunday. I was standing during worship, and we were singing songs about God's awesomeness and majesty, and suddenly I was drawn back to the last time I saw you and Rex at the funeral home. I could picture the room and the people, and Todd, lying there so peacefully. Then I had a glorious picture of him (Todd) in heaven, more alive than ever, happy, joyful, singing, sharing his music with the angels."

Life as we know it has changed profoundly and will probably keep changing for a long while. Some of the changes will enlarge our souls, equipping us to help others. Some will torment us for a season. Some will push us deeper and transform us in ways that better reflect both the character and the compassion of Jesus. That's good. But overarching all of this is *what hasn't changed.* The promises of God have not changed. Jesus has not resigned His job as the heavenly Intercessor who ever lives to pray—He's still at the Father's right hand praying for me and for you. The devil hasn't changed. He's still the father of lies, intent on killing, stealing, and destroying. The battle hasn't changed. Our need to engage in spiritual warfare remains critical, and we are more in need of wearing our spiritual armor than ever before. God's presence in my life hasn't changed. His promise to never leave me or forsake me is the same. The power of prayer hasn't changed. What E.M. Bounds said many years ago rings in my ears. "God shapes the world by prayer. Prayers are deathless...they live before God and God's heart is set on them...prayers outlive the lives of those who uttered them, outlive a generation, outlive an age, outlive a WORLD." He's right, and that hasn't changed. The important things, the eternal things have not changed.[6]

People ask Connie how she *feels,* and she responds with what she *knows* to be true. God is faithful, kind, powerful, good, near, caring, and helpful, and He is able to make all things, even hard things, work together for our good.

Inhabit Praise

The Bible declares, "For in him *we live* and *move* and *have* our being" (Acts 17:28 NIV). The Contemporary English Version says, "He gives us the power to live, to move, and to be who we are" (CEV). I like to begin many of my retreat messages to my after-40 sisters with Colossians 1:17, "He is before all things, and in Him all things hold together." The Bible also tells us that "His divine power has granted to us *everything* pertaining to life and godliness" (2 Peter 1:3). In Christ we have it all!

So why doesn't it feel like it sometimes? I think the most common reason is that we are not proclaiming our status to ourselves, to each other, or to Satan, who seeks to discourage us. I love the psalm that says, "Thou art holy, O thou that inhabitest the praises of Israel" (Psalm 22:3 KJV). God inhabits the praises of His people. It's as if God sits down to listen whenever we take time to worship Him.

I have found that the harder life gets, the louder I praise, and the louder I praise, the easier life becomes. So I buy worship music and play it in my home and in my car. I go to church and worship with others who also sing praise to God.

Years ago I was studying Philippians 4, a passage all about finding joy and peace. Something we all want, right? As I studied what many of the words meant in their original language, a picture came to mind. Let me see if I can explain it. First, here are the verses:

> Rejoice in the Lord always; again I will say, rejoice! Let your gentle spirit be known to all men. The Lord is near. Be anxious for nothing, but in everything by prayer and supplication with thanksgiving let your requests be made known to God. And the peace of God, which surpasses all comprehension, will guard your hearts and your minds in Christ Jesus. Finally, [sisters], whatever is true, whatever is honorable, whatever is right, whatever is pure, whatever is lovely, whatever is of good repute, if there is any excellence and if anything worthy of praise, dwell on these things. The things you have learned and received and heard and seen in me, practice these things, and the God of peace will be with you (Philippians 4:4-9).

How do we get "the peace of God"? In my mind, I take that fear, frustration, or concern that is bothering me, and I wrap it in the tissue paper of prayer. I then present my "supplication" (the request) "with thanksgiving." Thanksgiving is the gift bag that transports the gift to God. I take care to wrap up the request and place it in a bag of thanksgiving because I realize *who* I am presenting the request to—the all-powerful, all-knowing, sovereign King of kings of the universe. It is only when we pray knowing to *whom* we pray that the peace comes. When I picture my request being placed into tissue paper, dropped into a gift bag, and presented before the throne of the God, who can do something about it, I gain hope!

Nearer

"Come *near* to God and he will come *near* to you" (James 4:8 NIV). When you come near to God, you are never the same. Daniel 11:32 says, "The people who know their God will display strength and take action." I want to be one who is strong and takes action. To do that, I believe that I also need to be like the psalmists, who say, "as the deer pants for the water brooks, so my soul pants for You, O God" (Psalm 42:1). When you long for God, you become a bold, brave woman.

How hungry are you for God? Do you want to see miracles in your life? The way to get God to show up is to fill your life with praise. Practicing praise is just like practicing the piano or dance. The more you practice, the better you get. Praise Him, sister!

Victory Think

Life after 40 can feel like a maze. Women who thrive have discovered that one way out of the confusion is to walk God's Word into your life by personalizing the Word of God. Praying personalized Scripture does many things:

1. It helps you see how the principles of truth can apply to your situation. "All Scripture is inspired by God and profitable for teaching, for reproof, for correction, for training in righteousness; so that the man of God may be adequate, equipped for every good work" (2 Timothy 3:16-17).

2. It illuminates the next step you should take. The psalmist says, "Your word is a lamp to my feet and a light to my path" (Psalm 119:105).

3. It is the power to pull down strongholds and create a path of promise out of the pain.

God's Word brings supernatural answers. It's not that praying God's Word strong-arms God. Praying God's Word simply helps us pray in closer accordance to God's heart.

To personalize Scripture to your situation, select a verse and then place yourself, or the person you are praying for, right in the middle of the passage. Here's one of my favorites from Psalm 91:1-5. I have added brackets around the words changed to personalize it to my life:

> [Pam], who dwells in the shelter of the Most High, will abide in the shadow of the Almighty. I will say to the LORD, "My refuge and my fortress, my God, in whom I trust!" For it is He who delivers [me] from the snare of the trapper...He will cover [me] with His pinions, and under His wings [I] may seek refuge; His faithfulness is a shield and bulwark. [I] will not be afraid.

I have seen the power of God's Word in women's lives. There is power in prayer to bring prodigals back to God, move husbands' hearts back home, bring back hope, navigate through unthinkable news, regain strength, and cope with health issues. More than anything else, God's Word gives us the power to hold our heads above the swirling waters of life change, fear, interpersonal conflict, or unthinkable circumstances.

I have asked Kathryn to share how her relationship with God pulled her through the unthinkable. Kathryn and I touched base numerous times over the dozens of months of her journey. She applied all the principles in this chapter, but she especially chose to proclaim God's Word over her life and her family's to gain the wisdom, strength, and hope she needed to move herself and her family through a circumstance no woman, no mother, would ever want to find herself in. I hope her story, written in her words, will bring you hope, no matter what you are facing today.

> Molestation. It shattered our life like a baseball smashing a picture window, leaving shards of jagged glass all about. It felt as though that baseball crashed through our life and hit me full force in the stomach. It knocked the wind out of me. It made me sick to my stomach. It left me numb and weak. My precious daughter...by her stepfather...

my husband. How impossible. How inconceivable. I was utterly and completely paralyzed.

Thankfully, God was not. Many years ago, He had begun placing in our lives the people my daughter and I would need to empower us, pray for and with us, and hold us up as we took one step, then a second step, and a third toward healing and forgiveness.

The moment our world shattered I cried out to the Lord "Noooooooo!" as I pulled my daughter to me and we sobbed together. I felt such guilt, such pain, such sorrow. In crying out to God in prayer, He responded with my pastor's name, a gifted man of God and longtime friend. A man who understands the pain sin brings upon a family. He knew what that first and second and third step should be and led us through each step, one by one.

God had provided a loving and caring youth leader for my daughter, to whom she first revealed this ugly, horrible experience. When she shared her story, she was also surrounded by her best and most trusted girlfriends. God was already providing a safe haven and support group for her.

My daughter and I thankfully had and still have an extremely close relationship and were able to comfort each other. But we also each needed our trusted friends and pastor to counsel us through. I feared my daughter would feel anger, even hatred, toward me for allowing this to happen to her, for bringing this man into our home. I hated myself for letting this happen.

God had also been creating cherished friendships in my life. Ladies I knew I could trust with this deep dark secret, who wouldn't judge, who wouldn't share my story with others. These sweet sisters in Christ walked, talked, prayed, and cried with me and often listened when I needed to talk and were just there with me when I needed someone close by.

Two months later my husband, in an effort to come clean, also confessed to me two affairs early on in our marriage. Slam! Another hit to the gut. But God gave me, through His Holy Spirit at the very moment of that announcement, the ability to forgive my husband. It is nothing I can explain. I felt literally compelled to offer my acceptance of his apologies and I truly forgave him. It was much later before I was able to forgive his sins against my daughter.

I told my husband to move out the night my daughter revealed the molestation. He was to have no contact with her. We talked to a police officer, child welfare professionals, counselors, and legal experts, and in the end, it was my daughter's decision to not pursue legal recourse.

Months later I agreed to meet my husband once a week at church. I was torn. I knew God hated what he had done to my daughter, and I knew God hated divorce. God gave me Jeremiah 29:11: "'I know the plans I have for you,' declares the LORD, 'plans to prosper you and not to harm you, plans to give you hope and a future.'" I was certain God did not want me to make a decision immediately to divorce. No one in my family (none of whom know God) understood this decision, and in human terms it made no sense. But I knew I was following God's direction for me. For a few months my husband truly repented and totally surrendered his life to God. God did an amazing work in him, and I saw that new creature born in my husband. Was God going to do a God-sized miracle in our family? Was He going to give me the husband I *thought* I had married and bring about healing and forgiveness in every family member who knew the story? Could He really redeem this ugliness?

Through the miraculous work of the Holy Spirit and much prayer, my daughter was able to forgive her stepfather. This freed her from the power he and the molestation held over her. However, she was not at all interested in having him back in her life. Over the next several months and what turned into two and a half years, my husband fell back into old habits and shed the new creature for the old.

I prayed to God, asking what I was to do. He responded that I was to take a step back from the situation and just observe my husband. Watch for indications that he was trustworthy and a new creation or not. Within 24 hours God opened my eyes to see that my husband was his old self and, therefore, not trustworthy. Within another two days, God made it clear that He was leading me to divorce my husband. Almost two years before this, God had prepared my heart and allowed me to see that my marriage could likely end in divorce. He promised He would give me peace about it, and that is exactly what I experienced. Joy? No. Peace? Yes.

Through the two and a half years of my waiting on God's direction, my dear prayer warrior friends did not judge me. They stood by me. Even though I'm sure many could not understand why I didn't file for divorce immediately, they believed in my relationship with God and believed I was listening to His leading. They encouraged me, prayed for me, and demonstrated God's *agape* love throughout this terrible yet redeemed experience.

I was still struggling with the decision to divorce. Then God gave me these verses in Proverbs 13:19-20: "A longing fulfilled is sweet to the soul, but fools detest turning from evil. He who walks with the wise grows wise, but a companion of fools suffers harm."

I would have been a companion of a fool and would have suffered harm had I stayed in the relationship once God opened my eyes to see that my husband was not turning from evil.

I had asked at one point, "Could God really redeem this ugliness?" The answer is, yes!

God made us creatures of choice. My husband missed
out on being part of a God-sized miracle. That was his
choice. My daughter and I, we chose redemption. We
have been able to use this experience to help those God
places in our paths, especially my daughter. Yes, our
Redeemer lives!

In the middle of a nightmare experience, Kathyrn has been
able to keep her career moving forward and serve God in ministry
and volunteer work. She has been able to raise amazing children,
including this precious, now grown daughter, who all love and serve
God despite the evil that Satan tried to use to destroy their home,
life, and family. Those around Kathryn credit her deep and personal
walk with God as the reason she is able to go on and go forward.
She digs into the Word, studies its meaning, prays daily, and asks
God to show her how to apply each piece as she reads and meditates
on it. She has many healthy patterns in her life, including a woman's
small-group Bible study, regular prayer walks with friends, weekly
worship and church attendance, and a heart to serve others, no
matter how much pain she found herself in. By keeping her upward
focus, Kathryn gained the ability to thrive despite circumstance
that could easily have led to depression or self-defeating choices.

Embrace the Future

Midlife is full of opportunities. When I was a little girl, I loved
to spend recess doing double Dutch jump rope. To be successful at
double Dutch (two ropes twirled by a person at each end, and you
run in between the ropes and jump in) required split-second timing
to enter. It was common to stand and move your arms in rhythm
with the ropes until you got the mesmerizing rhythm down pat so
you could jump in and not trip. Sometimes I'd stand for a long time
on the sideline, warming up to the idea of entry.

As I approached 40, I felt as though I were again standing on
the sidelines trying to get in rhythm to enter. I met 40 with mixed
emotions. I was excited because I felt comfortable in my own skin
and I felt that I knew my place in society. I had gained a measure

of success with my marriage, my kids, and in my career, so I felt as though I had a trump card. You know—the upper hand (for once)! I felt a little like the character in the movie *Fried Green Tomatoes* when she is battling for a parking spot and crashes her car into a younger driver's vying for the same spot. The older of the two shouts out: "I am older, wiser, and have better insurance."

Studies show midlife and beyond can be a positive experience: 100 years ago the average age of menopause in a woman in Britain was 47, but the life expectancy of British women was only 49. "Now women become menopausal at just over 50, but life expectancy is nearer 80, so we can expect to spend 25 or 30 years after menopause...The survey, called the Jubilee women study, asked women over 50 to compare their lives with those of women their age 50 years ago. Three-quarters said their health was better and that they had more fun, while 93% said they had more independence; all felt they had more choice in everything from work to leisure pursuits."[7] "Most women say their lives improve after the onset of the menopause, according to research published today showing the fiftysomethings are happier, healthier, and have better sex lives than when younger. A survey of women aged 50-64 found 65% said they were happier than before the menopause, 66% felt more independent, and 59% were enjoying better relationships with partners and friends. Asked about working lives, 48% claimed an improvement since the menopause, compared with 15% reporting deterioration. Although 19% said their sex life was less satisfactory, they were outnumbered by the 29% who said it got better."[8]

If you relive regret, people's ungratefulness, or any of the other hurtful things people did to you in the past, you can become negative, bitter, and harsh—and then no one will want to be around you. My friends Jack and Robin once said to me, "Life is too short to live looking in the rearview mirror." But if you focus forward and look to God to create the next great opportunity, you will discover more hope and happiness that is abundant. My goal for the second half of life is stated on a poster I created and placed on my wall:

Not that I have already obtained all this, or have already been made perfect, but I press on to take hold of that for which Christ Jesus took hold of me. Brothers, I do not consider myself yet to have taken hold of it. But one thing I do: Forgetting what is behind and straining toward what is ahead, I press on toward the goal to win the prize for which God has called me heavenward in Christ Jesus (Philippians 3:12-14 NIV).

— *Joy Choice* —

Which one of the secrets to successfully THRIVE do you want to begin implementing? Select one and go out today and buy, or create, something that will help you accomplish working one step into your daily routine.

For my forty-fourth birthday, I asked my friends for a "present of God's presence." I asked for a verse of hope I could post, memorize, and meditate on. Here are a few of my favorites. Perhaps one might encourage you as you embrace a change in your own life.

- Forget the former things; do not dwell in the past. See, I am doing a new thing...I am making a way in the desert and streams in the wasteland (Isaiah 43:18-19).

- Do not be afraid or discouraged...For the battle is not yours but God's... Go out to face them tomorrow, and the LORD will be with you (2 Chronicles 20:15,17).

- The eyes of the LORD are on those who fear him, on those whose hope is in his unfailing love...he is our help and our shield...May your unfailing love rest upon us, O LORD, even as we put our hope in you (Psalm 33:18,20,22 NIV).

4

Get Moving

*Physical fitness is the first requisite of
happiness…If at the age of 30 you are stiff
and out of shape, you are old. If at 60 you
are supple and strong, then you are young.*

A friend e-mailed me her exercise program:

For my birthday this year, my husband purchased a
week of private lessons at the local health club for me.
Although I am still in great shape since playing on my
high school softball team, I decided it would be a good
idea to go ahead and give it a try.

I called the club and made my reservations with a personal trainer named Tony, who identified himself as a
26-year-old aerobics instructor and model for athletic
clothing and swimwear.

My husband seemed pleased with my enthusiasm to get
started. The club encouraged me to keep a diary to chart
my progress.

Monday: Started my day at 6:00 AM. Tough to get out of
bed but found it was well worth it when I arrived at the
health club to find Tony waiting for me. He is something
of a god with blond hair, dancing eyes, and a dazzling
white smile. WOO HOO!!!

Tony gave me a tour and showed me the machines. He
took my pulse after five minutes on the treadmill. He

was alarmed that my pulse was so fast, but I attribute it to standing next to all those rippling muscles. Tony was encouraging as I did my sit-ups, although my gut was already aching from holding it in when he was around. This is going to be a FANTASTIC week!!!

Tuesday: I drank a whole pot of coffee, but I finally made it out of the door. Tony made me lie on my back and push a heavy iron bar into the air...then he put weights on it! My legs were a little wobbly on the treadmill, but I made the full mile. Tony's rewarding smile made it all worthwhile. I feel GREAT!! It's a whole new life for me.

Wednesday: The only way I can brush my teeth is by laying the toothbrush on the counter and moving my mouth back and forth over it. I believe I have a hernia in both pectorals. Driving was OK as long as I didn't try to steer or stop...Tony was impatient with me, insisting that my screams bothered the other club members. (His voice is a little too perky for early in the morning, and when he scolds, he gets this nasally whine that is VERY annoying.) My chest hurt when I got on the treadmill, so Tony put me on the StairMaster. Why would anyone invent a machine to simulate an activity rendered obsolete by elevators? Tony told me it would help me get in shape and enjoy life. Right.

Thursday: Tony was waiting for me with his vampirelike teeth exposed as his thin, cruel lips were pulled back in a full snarl. I couldn't help being a half hour late. It took that long for me to tie my shoes. Tony took me to work out with dumbbells. When he wasn't looking, I ran and hid in the ladies' room. He sent Barbie to find me. Then, as punishment, he put me on the rowing machine... which I sank.

Friday: I hate that Tony more than any human being has ever hated any other human being in the history of the world. Stupid, skinny, puffed-up peacock! If there was a part of my body I could move without unbearable pain, I would beat him with it. Tony wanted me to work on my triceps. I don't have any triceps! And if you don't want dents in the floor, don't hand me barbells or anything that weighs more than a sandwich. The treadmill flung me off and I landed on a PE teacher. Why couldn't it have been someone softer, like a drama coach or choir director?

Saturday: Tony left a message on my answering machine in his grating, shrill voice wondering why I did not show up today. Just hearing him made me want to smash the machine. However, I lacked the strength even to use the TV remote and ended up watching eleven straight hours of the Weather Channel.

Sunday: I'm having the church van pick me up for services today so I can go and thank God that this week is over. I will also pray that next year my husband will choose a gift for me that is fun...like a root canal or a mammogram.[1]

A New Attitude

Does the fictional account above capture how you feel about exercise? I have always had a love/hate relationship with working out. In my youth I was a gymnast, dancer, and cheerleader. One semester while I was on the college diving team, I took five PE classes at the same time plus taught gymnastics each afternoon. I even rode my bike to work many days! Then I married my husband, got pregnant, and was put on bed rest for the last six weeks of my pregnancy. I was then rewarded with a six-week postpartum recovery from a C-section. Through all that I gained 70 pounds of "baby fat." Armed with optimism under all that postpartum tummy, I went back to my first aerobics class. I thought to myself, *I'm an athlete. No problem.*

Problem! The next day I couldn't even get out of bed! The seeds of an "exercise is hard work" attitude were planted that day—and I have been recovering from my bad attitude ever since. Trying to be an informed woman in my forties, I ran across some startling stats:

- On average, women gain about a pound a year during the years leading up to menopause.[2]

- Fifty percent of all women in America over 45 are classified as overweight.[3]

- Beginning as early as age 35, we lose 7 pounds of muscle each decade, and by the time we are 65 we can lose as much as 65 percent of our ability to do physical activity.[4]

- As many as 12% of all deaths in the U.S. may be attributed indirectly to lack of regular physical activity.[5]

These numbers got my attention and I was motivated to change, especially after one particular day when my son said, "Mom, if you don't start running again, you will die, and I don't want you to die of a heart attack like Grandpa did." I have since repented of my "no run" policy—and I actually run on occasion with my track running son! I stuff my pride, and I tell myself, "Think thin!" I ask myself questions like: *What do thin people do?* (They are active.) *What do thin people eat?* (Food that is healthy and in small portions.) *How do thin people have fun?* (They dance, jog with friends, swim, play tennis, bike along the boardwalk, take the stairs, surf, ski, play handball, go to the health club, park far away from the store and walk, run along the beach, walk to the corner market.) Thin people do active stuff *for fun!* So, if I remember exercise is *fun,* I get motivated. It's all in the way you look at it! How about you? Can you join me in having some *fun?*

Thinking thin and ordering my priorities to "have more fun" felt weird at first because I had so trained myself to put everyone in the world and their needs before my own as a mom. (I read a stat that said only four percent of baby boomers put themselves first—so I know I am not alone in this.)[6] But if I wanted to continue being an active mom, and be an active grandmother in the future, I needed to put taking care of me and my body higher on the list. This wasn't selfishness; it was smart, strategic thinking. By thinking *thin,* you can move toward thin. I am way beyond believing the unrealistic illusion that the world needs more runway models, but I want to "think thin" because if I am my target weight, I will live longer. I am going for longevity, not beauty and glamour, at this point in my life. I personally think it is beautiful to be *breathing, moving, and living!* Girlfriend, if we are going to live longer and stronger, we have got to get moving.

Time to Play

You might be wondering, as I did one day when I got on the scale shortly after my fortieth birthday, *What happened to me?* My defeat in the battle of the bulge happened slowly, gradually, and silently over a decade. Little by little I noticed that my kids got more active and I got more responsible (that is, sedentary). Year after year I drove them to numerous sports practices and I sat on way too many benches waiting while they exercised. Shortly after my forty-third birthday, the doctor confirmed my suspicions and announced to me, "Pam, you have *high* glucose, *high* cholesterol, and are living at *high* risk." Something drastic needed to happen. I needed to learn to play again! Brrrrinnnnnggggg! The recess bell has rung—let's have some fun!

Four Simple Steps to Getting Active

To live a *Fantastic After 40!* life, you will want to take great care of your body and get movin'! There is a four-prong approach to getting physically fit (with recommended time input for "fantastic" fitness):

AEROBIC	STRETCH/BALANCE
30 minutes–1 hour	10–20 minutes
5-6/week	Every day
WEIGHT	**CORE WORK**
Resistance Workout	(Pilates)
3/week	2-3/week recommended

Core work

At age 86 Joseph Hubertus Pilates, the founder of the Pilates exercise program that works on core body strength, declared this: "I must be right. Never an aspirin. Never injured a day in my life. The whole country, the whole world, should be doing my exercises. They'd be happier."[7] Pilates appears to have been a frail child, suffering from asthma, rickets, and rheumatic fever. His drive to overcome these ailments led him to become a gymnast, diver, and skier. At the outbreak of WWI, Pilates was placed under forced internment along with other German nationals. There he taught fellow camp members the exercises he had developed. It was at this time that he began devising the system of original exercises known today as mat work, or exercises done on the floor. Later, he was transferred to another camp, where he became a caretaker to many internees struck with wartime disease and physical injury. There he devised equipment to rehabilitate his "patients," creating spring resistance movement for the bedridden.

After the war Pilates returned to Germany, where he trained the police before immigrating to the United States. He opened a "body-conditioning studio" with his wife, Clara, in New York City. Through his writings and his students, his method was passed on after his death in 1967 at the age of 87.[8]

Practiced faithfully, Pilates yields numerous benefits:

- Increased lung capacity and circulation through deep, healthy breathing
- Strength and flexibility, particularly of the abdomen and back muscles
- Improved posture, reduced back pain
- Increased balance
- Core strengthening
- Bone density and joint health improvement
- Increased flexibility

- An awareness of and strengthened dynamic stability

- Improved coordination

- Reduced stress[9]

If you were (are) a ballerina, gymnast, or dancer, you are most likely familiar with Pilates exercises, as most of the warm-ups for these exercise arts contain elements of Pilates. Basic core work strengthens stomach muscles, thus giving the lower back and major muscle groups in legs and torso the power they need for the daily activities of standing, walking, and general movement.

There are other core exercise options, including DVDs, ballet bar work, a workout atop a large rubber ball, and water aerobics classes. One can learn the basics of core work relatively inexpensively from any simple DVD or class where you can follow an instructor along until you have the basics memorized and can do them on your own. The positive outcome is that strengthening your core gives you the ability to stay active and independent.

Resistance

Weight-bearing physical activity (such as walking, running, dancing, and weight training) reduces the rate of bone loss and protects remaining bone tissue. Some of the benefits include:

- Increased muscle strength, power, endurance, and size

- Increased bone density and strength, reducing fracture risk if you happen to fall in everyday life. Bone mass is increased, reducing the risk of the bone-thinning disease, osteoporosis.

- Reduced body fat and increased muscle-to-fat ratio

- Boosted metabolism

- Lowered heart rate and blood pressure after exercise (thought to reduce the risk of heart disease)

- Improved balance and stability

- Enhanced performance of everyday tasks

- Reduced risk of developing negative medical conditions—for example, diabetes and arthritis

- Improved posture from abdominal work, which may reduce chronic lower back pain

- Better self-esteem and confidence

Resistance training can be done in several ways. The use of resistance machines, free weights (dumbbells and barbells), rubber tubing, or your own body weight as in doing push-ups, sit-ups, squats, bar dips, or abdominal crunches are all effective. A full circuit of resistance-training machines is nice, but all you really need is a carpeted floor and some weighted objects. You can even use a phone book, bags of rice, soup cans, or liters of soda.

Start each resistance training session with a 5- to 15-minute aerobic warm-up and end with a cooldown. Women should not be fearful of resistance training. It will not turn you into a bodybuilder with bulging muscles. Resistance training can become your new best friend because it helps you burn more calories *at rest* (even while you sleep!). Johns Hopkins researchers say that while aerobic exercise burns more calories as it is being done, the metabolism slows back down to normal after about half an hour. "Women who perform resistance training, however, burn more calories for two hours after their workouts."[10] So to combat a slowing metabolism, lift weights.

Loss of muscle mass typically begins in one's thirties or forties and continues, even for women who take hormone replacement. As muscles shrink, fat takes their place, and that process leads to a slowdown in metabolism and weight gain, even if caloric intake and expenditure remain the same. Weight training can reverse this process, putting back muscle (which uses more calories and takes up less room than fat) and diminishing fat stores. So even if you lose no pounds, by strengthening your muscles *you can lose inches and sizes.*

The easiest way to begin resistance training is to make an appointment at a credible health club and have a personal trainer design a program specifically for you and your goals. Are you ready to hit the gym?

Bend and Flex

Improving range of motion and flexibility will remedy stiffness and soreness that are common as we reach menopause. I have found it helpful to stretch every morning after I wake and anytime during the day I feel stiffness setting in. I also rest better if I stretch a little before I climb into bed at night. I started to write down all the ways I stretch in my 10- to 30-minute daily morning routine, but writing it out would take many pages. Besides, I think it is easier to learn these stretches when they are demonstrated for you. Look into the following resources to get up to speed: a health club instructor; *Praise Moves* or *Yoga for Christians* DVD; a friend who has a background in dance, gymnastics, or ballet; or a cable TV exercise program that incorporates stretching elements.

Start with what you remember from basic ballet class or PE class "calisthenics," and you will be headed in the right direction. I have always stretched, so if you travel, you can easily spot me in the airport. I am the lady traveling in "Chico's wear" doing stretches and lunges on the floor next to the gate. I can still do the splits at 48! (My goal is the splits till my grave!)

Stretching also keeps my posture strong and me in tune with my body. Daily stretches keep me out of the chiropractor's office and have drastically improved my battle with migraines. Overall, I begin my stretches laying on my back soon after I wake up. I simply breathe from the diaphragm. I like to place my hand on my tummy and feel the air go deeply in and out, and I picture it going up and down my spine or body core. I often meditate on Scripture. "In him (God) we live and move and have our being" (Acts 17:28 NIV). A disciplined practice of deep breathing will also lower stress and add to your overall cardio health.

I then move to stretches. I do sitting stretches, followed by ones I do while kneeling or lunging, then I move to stretches I can do while standing. I try to "wake up" my muscles first.

To be honest, most of us would be moving the right direction if we just turned on our favorite music and moved to the music the way we did in kindergarten. Sway like a tree, spin like a twirling wind chime, pose like a warrior, bow before God as though we really are capturing His majesty, and reach up and out as though we are trying to grab that brass ring!

All Options Are Not the Same

All movement is God's movement, but not all thoughts are God's thoughts. What do I mean by this? God is the Creator. He designed our bodies and says they are "fearfully and wonderfully made" (Psalm 139:14). In the psalms we are encouraged to praise God. This means that reaching up your arms to heaven, bowing before God the Creator, as well as any movement that tunes up our body, is holy movement. So all the stretches, all the poses, all the ballet moves and dances steps, any stretch found in a yoga class, Tai chi, martial arts, Pilates, or aerobics class are all God's.

However, not all teachers and their words *are lined up with God's Word.* That is why even though yoga has many wonderful benefits, I can't just give a blanket endorsement of it as a method to increase flexibility and balance. This is because yoga and other Eastern exercise movements are parts of belief systems. While the movements of the body themselves are quite benign and neutral, and even predate the philosophy of yoga, often the teachers of these movements hook them to the belief systems of Eastern religions which contain teachings that oppose the Bible. The Bible says there is one God, the Creator of heaven and earth. It also explains that this God, in His infinite love, sent His Son down to earth. This Son, Jesus, lived a perfect life and then gave up that life and was crucified on the cross for our imperfections (sins). We can either choose to walk away from that love and that gift, or we can choose to embrace that love and gift and decide to personally receive Jesus Christ as our Savior and Lord of our life. If we have made the choice for Jesus, that means we choose to walk away from other belief systems or gods. The teachings of yoga and a few other Eastern martial arts contain philosophies that are in direct opposition to Jesus and the Bible.

Can we redeem the movement and extricate the beliefs that are not in line with the truths of the Bible? Sure we can. Some videos and books may contain *only* the movements and not the philosophies, which are safer spiritually for us. In a class setting, you would need to know the teacher, his or her philosophy, and how much Eastern thought they will bring into the class (or preferably, how much they are purposefully leaving out). Some rare teachers have

One-Hour Renewals

- Take a prayer walk.

- Take a bike ride.

- Arrange for a massage (to trim time, have the masseuse come to your office or home).

- Have a pedicure or manicure.

- Have a facial or give yourself a facial.

- Call your husband home for lunch and have a "quickie" in the bedroom.

- Walk by the lake or at the beach or up to the top of a hill for a scenic view. Even climbing the stairs to the top of a building with a view will do for a change of scenery.

- Have a back facial. (Just a little FYI: Often all these spa treatments can be received at a fraction of the price at a local cosmetology school.)

- Take a dance class, stretch class, Pilates, or aerobics class or do one of these to a video at home to keep it well under an hour.

- Take a bubble bath or sit in a Jacuzzi.

- Read a book or watch an uplifting video or TV show.

taken the religion out of yoga and other movement classes, thus making them more neutral. And even rarer still is the teacher who is a Christian who has taken the movements and added in the truth and Scripture from the Bible. One new movement that is sweeping the nation is led by Laurette Willis, the founder of Praise Moves, which is seeking to redeem the movement of yoga but replaces the names of the positions with words that better reflect a Christian faith.[11] Susan Bordenkircher, author of *Yoga for Christians* learned that there are approximately 15 million people in this country practicing yoga, and fully 50 to 60 percent of them say they come from a church background. She took a bold move and combined the poses of yoga with Christian meditations in an "Outstretched Worship" class. Personally, I took a stretch class from a pastor's daughter who had tried to do something similar. In class were the movements of yoga, but she extricated out the philosophy and interjected in scriptural truths like "cast your cares upon God for He cares for you," "God is a very present help in time of need," etc. This way we could rest and relax in God's presence, power, and provision instead of constantly having to process and be on guard mentally and spiritually in a regular yoga class taught by someone who believed in Eastern thought.

I don't believe in throwing the baby out with the bathwater (never doing the stretch movements), but I am also very intent on focusing on what is true because the truth will set me free (John 8:32). Each morning I put on my praise music (some great Scripture set to music can be ordered at: firstplace.org/scripture.html) and then do a series of stretches to loosen my joints, stretch my muscles, build my core, improve my balance, and lower my stress. Because I am in control of what I hear and what I see, I can truly relax. By stretching to Scripture-based praise music each morning, I gain the physical benefits of exercise, the emotional confidence that comes from being connected to God, and the inner spiritual power that comes from meditating on the truth of the Bible. Now that's how I want to begin my day—with confidence!

Build Your Balance

Unfortunately, age impacts balance. In order to prevent nasty, embarrassing falls, practice a few simple balance moves, even one per day as you are going about your day. Try one of these:

- When doing dishes, rise up on your toes while holding on to the cupboard. Then let go of the cupboard with your hands and stand steady. Repeat.

- Stand next to a wall, lift your outside leg up in front of you off the floor slightly, hold, let go of wall. Repeat, both sides. (This can be done with a variety of positions: bended knee held up; grab ankle and hold up in a stretch; arabesque (ballet) pose with leg extended back and chest and body lowered toward floor; etc.)

- Be a tree (this one looks like a martial arts move). With one leg bent so that your foot rests on the knee of other leg and is turned out, extend your arms upward like tree branches.

- Bend at your waist and sweep the floor with your hands and swing up to the other side to stand upright again. Make the top half of your body move in a circle. Repeat both directions.

- Be a kid. Walk on a curb as though it were a balance beam.

- Sit on a fitness ball and lift your feet. Try to balance while sitting.

- Do a simple pirouette turn like a ballerina and "spot" by looking at a spot eye level ahead and keep your eyes on the spot and quickly turn your head to maintain eye contact as you do your turn.

- Using a table or any flat surface about waist level, place one outstretched leg up as if on a ballet bar. Raise and lower yourself on the standing leg. Bend and stretch forward onto the outstretched leg.

Aerobic Activity

Aerobic, or cardio, exercises are those that increase your heart rate. Choices can include brisk walking, aerobic dance, or biking. Some trendy cardio classes are available in DVD form—just watch infomercials for a wide selection. Swimming is excellent cardio care because it is gentle on the joints. Water aerobics is a nice option to vary your pool or aerobic time. Anything that gets your heart rate up for at least 20 minutes is doing a good job at moving you toward fitness. Menopausal women should aim for 20 to 60 minutes of aerobic exercise most days of the week—give yourself Sunday off from aerobic activity if you'd like, but try for some cardio pumping activity the other five or six days a week. By far the easiest and cheapest place to begin is by walking.

Almost half of women are walking for exercise on a regular basis.[12] One study found that 49 of 50 people who lost 30 pounds or more walked for at least half an hour at a brisk pace every day.[13] Walking briskly for 3 hours a week can reduce your risk of heart disease by 40 to 50 percent.[14] So, sister, get your tennies on and walk as if you are 10 minutes late for an appointment! And in all the fuss over taking care of your body, choose joy! I saw a sign in a health club that read:

> *I signed up for an exercise class and was told to wear*
> *loose-fitting clothing. If I HAD any loose-fitting clothing,*
> *I wouldn't have signed up in the first place!*

— Joy Choice —

Get active! Complete the fitness quadrant chart on page 77. Set a goal and write how you are going to do each one of those areas, one per day this first week. Then select a reward off the "Personal Party" rejuvenation list and reward yourself for getting active after you complete today's exercise!

Time to Party!

The rest can be the best. What activities have you always wanted to try but were too busy cooking, doing laundry, or running the carpool to do? Whittle away on these secret hopes and dreams while you launch your children into college, and as more and more time frees up, try more new activities. Have you ever wanted to ballroom dance, kayak, mountain climb? How do you lower your stress on a daily basis? In my book *The 10 Best Decisions a Woman Can Make,* I encourage "Personal Parties" which are daily vacation moments that can lower your stress and be the rewards you give yourself for eating well (instead of a hot fudge sundae reward, buy a new magazine and sit in the hammock for 20 minutes). Instead of munching on that bag of chips, reward yourself with one of the following "Personal Parties."

- Put on your favorite music (jazz, classical, or instrumental harp, violin, soft piano, etc.). Take deep breaths, close your eyes, and sink back in your favorite chair.

- Walk around the block while wearing your iPod. Play a favorite uplifting tune into your ears and let it sink into your heart.

- Put on praise music, especially songs that are God's Word set to music. Take a walk, stretch, or dance to the music for a few moments.

- Give yourself a mini massage. Roll your neck and shoulders forward, and then circle your arms forward and back. Reach over your head to one side and then to the other, then touch your toes.

- Play a game on the computer.

- Take a walk to a courtyard or nearby park—or even a rooftop. Get some fresh air.

- Read a devotional or inspirational book or listen to an inspiring CD.

- Send an e-mail to your husband, your child, or friend. Taking your eyes off yourself and focusing on someone else and their issues can make yours seem smaller.

- Look through a photo album.

- Call a friend and ask her to pray with you.

- Buy some flowers for your desk or grab an orange or fruit smoothie and stop to eat it.

- Keep an eye mask in the fridge. Stop what you are doing, lay back, and relax with this cool eye mask on your eyes.

- Sit in a comfortable place and close your eyes. Open and close one hand, then the other. Bend your elbow and relax on each side. Shrug your shoulders and breathe slow deep breaths. Picture yourself lying on your bed, on a sandy beach, or in a daisy-filled meadow.

- Pray through what is stressing you. Tell yourself, "God is in control." Hold up your hands and open your palms to let the stress go. Release the issue from your hands and give it to God's heart and hands.

Check Up On Yourself

*To change and to change for the
better are two different things.*

After I turned 40, my arms suddenly grew so short I couldn't read
the phone book very well. The print was irritatingly small. So I got
bifocals. One of my friends knew that I was a little distraught over
this new age marker in my life, so she zipped off the following e-
mail to me (in 18-point font size).

> Pam,
>
> Welcome to the ranks of the perimenopausal. Life will
> be changing, but don't worry. Arm yourself with a good
> sense of humor, and you'll be fine. After all, in today's
> world all kinds of things are changing (see attached).
>
> Love,
> Menopausal and making it

What was attached? "Even Barbie's Changing."

> *Bifocals Barbie:* Comes with her own set of blended-lens
> fashion frames in six wild colors (half-frames too!), neck
> chain, and large-print editions of *Vogue* and *Martha
> Stewart Living.*
>
> *Hot Flash Barbie:* Press Barbie's belly button and watch her
> face turn beet red while tiny drops of perspiration appear
> on her forehead! With handheld fan and tiny tissues.

Facial Hair Barbie: See Barbie's whiskers grow! Available with teensy tweezers and magnifying mirror.

Cook's Arms Barbie: Hide Barbie's droopy triceps with these new, roomier-sleeved gowns. Good news on the tummy front too: Muumuus are back! Cellulite cream and loofah sponge optional.

No More Wrinkles Barbie: Erase those pesky crow's-feet and lip lines with a tube of Skin Sparkle Spackle from Barbie's own line of exclusive age-blasting cosmetics.

Midlife Crisis Barbie: It's time to ditch Ken. Barbie needs a change, and Bruce (her personal trainer) is just what the doctor ordered. Comes with Prozac. They're hopping in her new red Miata and heading for the Napa Valley to open a B&B. Also comes with real tape of "Breaking Up Is Hard to Do."

Divorce Barbie: This one comes with Ken's car, Ken's house, and Ken's boat!

Obviously, these are all a joke. Mattel isn't changing their doll. But, doll, *we are changing,* and only a good sense of humor will get us through.

Ever-Changing You

You would think we women would be accustomed to change by now. Think back. Life, hormones, and emotions are fairly stable in a little girl's life. But womanhood is a different journey altogether. Just about the time we are ready to give up the backyard swing, we exchange it for an emotional swing kicked off by menstruation. We spend our teen years trying to stabilize the erratic emotions that spring up once a month, just to fall in love, marry, and experience pregnancy! Your husband may wonder, *What happened to my sweet wife, who once sat beside me, stroking my forehead and listening to my problems, who now sends me out for pickles and sets me up in a no-win situation by asking, "Am I fat?"*

But praise God that in the middle of pregnancy, your hormones do you a favor and, in spite of the size of your tummy, your libido kicks into high gear, and your husband never looked so good! Then, just as suddenly, your hormones shift again, and you can't even imagine wanting to take off your muumuu for sex or any other reason. This frustration peaks during the transitional phase of delivery with a tribal-like shriek: "Look what you did to me!" Fortunately, that anger is short-lived, and the new baby causes you to enter into a new state of happiness—except that many women fall prey to baby blues or postpartum depression. Eventually, our hormones return to their normal spontaneity, and we adjust to motherhood, over and over again.

Then, sometime during our childbearing years, usually between the ages of 28 and 38, when we get a moment to reflect, a midlife transition hits and we ask, "Why am I here? What is my purpose in life?" Just about the time we figure ourselves out, we are greeted by the perimenopause and menopause roller coaster. With enough TLC, supplements, medication, and family understanding, we can enjoy a semi-sane last leg of life. So only at the very beginning of life, when we are too young to appreciate it, and at the end of life, when we are too old to do much with it, are we emotionally stable.

That means women must *embrace change* as a friend. Biology does affect us, but it doesn't have to enslave us. Change is easier to embrace if we know what to expect and what might help us manage it.

The Meno Mama

More than 4800 women are entering menopause in the United States every day. Perimenopause is the 2- to 15-year-span prior to menopause. For some women the perimenopause period may be short—only a year or two. For others it may be as long as 7 to 10 years or even more. Some women in their late thirties and early forties may begin to show symptoms. The majority of women will begin to notice symptoms between 40 and 50. Twenty-five percent of women do not have any problems with menopause and manage the transition without assistance; 50 percent of women experience some menopausal symptoms, varying from mild to moderate. Twenty-five percent of women have more severe problems.[1]

The average age for American women to enter menopause is 51. However, it can occur anytime between a woman's late thirties and her late fifties. The term "menopause" comes from two Greek words that mean "month" and "to end." Menopause is the absence of menstruation for 12 months. Menopause also occurs when a woman's uterus and ovaries are surgically removed.

When a woman is approaching the end of her monthly cycles, she begins to experience an imbalance in her hormones. Perimenopause is the time before menopause when levels of estrogen and progesterone decline. For some women, perimenopause can be worse than actual menopause itself.

Signs That You Might Be Experiencing Menopause

You sell your home heating system at a yard sale. (Hot flashes)

Your husband complains about snow piling up on the bed. (Night sweats)

Your husband jokes that instead of buying a woodstove, he is using you to heat the family room this winter. Rather than just saying you are not amused, you shoot him. (Mood swing)

You write your kids' names on Post-it Notes. (Memory loss)

Your husband chirps, "Hi, honey, I'm home," and you reply, "Well, if it isn't Ozzie 'he never takes out the trash or calls when he is going to be late' Nelson." (Irritability)

You find guacamole in your hair after a Mexican dinner. (Fatigue)

You change your underwear after every sneeze. (Mild incontinence)

You need the Jaws of Life to help you out of your car after returning home from an Italian restaurant. (Sudden weight gain)

You ask Jiffy Lube to put you up on a hoist. (Dryness)

You take a sudden interest in Wrestle Mania. (Female hormone deficiency)

You're on so much estrogen that your husband of 35 years, who has a receding hairline, an extending beltline, and is standing in his ripped undershirt with a wrench in his hand, looks sexier than Brad Pitt, Mel Gibson, and Ricky Martin all rolled into one. (Hormone therapy)

Not funny, you say? Okay, the real symptoms are not as comical because they are real and can be a constant source of irritation. Your body (and your moods) may be changing so much that you barely recognize yourself. During true menopause, estrogen and progesterone levels are low and fairly constant. However, during perimenopause, hormone levels may fluctuate in an irregular pattern. Signs of perimenopause include:

Hot flashes. The sense of warmth starts suddenly, usually over your face, neck, and chest. Hot flashes are experienced by up to two-thirds of perimenopausal women. Hot flashes usually occur one to five years before the end of menstruation. These symptoms are more severe in women who have had their ovaries surgically removed. Hormonal changes trick the body into thinking it is too hot. To cool itself, blood is rushed to the surface of the skin, resulting in a flushed appearance.

Night sweats. Hot flashes that can interfere with sleep.

Cold flashes. Sudden chills that make you feel clammy.

Vaginal dryness, itching, and irritation. Lowered estrogen levels cause the lining of the vagina to become drier and thinner. This may lead to painful intercourse and decreased interest in sexual relations.

Urinary tract infections. The need to urinate frequently, burning on urination, itching in the urethra area.

Urinary incontinence. This can occur especially upon sneezing and laughing. The uterus and bladder slip lower into the pelvis. Urinary leakage may be related to pelvic floor changes that occurred years ago during labor and delivery. As the estrogen level drops, further changes can occur. Low estrogen levels may weaken the urethral sphincter that helps hold in urine. (Doing the Kegel exercises you learned in pregnancy may help.)

Osteoporosis. Bone density loss occurs when estrogen diminishes to a low level. The most rapid bone loss occurs during the first ten years of menopause.

Rising heart rate. Estrogen helped to dilate the arteries. Menopausal women are at greater risk of heart attacks.

Skin changes and increase in wrinkles. Decreasing estrogen levels make the skin less elastic.

Mood changes and irritability. Mood swings, sudden tears, and even rage may be more common, and more likely in women who have had difficulty with PMS. Estrogen levels may influence the production of serotonin. Serotonin is the hormone that makes women feel happy. Lowered levels lead to depression and other negative emotions.

Insomnia. Trouble sleeping is a common complaint of women in perimenopause or menopause itself. Night sweats may disrupt sleep. Irritability and depression can impair sleep.

Irregular periods. Periods may become shorter or longer, lighter or heavier. Phantom periods may occur. Cramping may increase or decrease. Eventually, menses lighten, become less frequent, and then stop.

Change in libido. A significant number of women report a decrease in sexual desire after the age of fifty. This is matched, however, by an equal number of women who report improved sexual desire. Competing influences in a woman's life vie for her sexual interest. Lower levels of estrogen and constant change in the way her body functions draws her interest down. At the same time, more time with her husband, a greater level of privacy, the absence of any worry of getting pregnant, and the increased maturity in her own spirit can make sexual activity more appealing.

Fatigue. This the most often named symptom of women in menopause.

Feelings of dread and anxiety. Feeling ill at ease or experiencing feelings of doom is not uncommon.

Difficulty concentrating, disorientation, and mental confusion. Some women experience difficulty with memory, attention span, concentration, or remembering specific words. A woman with attention deficit disorder may first come for treatment at this age because declining estrogen levels have exacerbated her ability to concentrate.

Itchy, crawly skin. The skin can feel as if ants were crawling under it.

Aching. Women often experience sore joints, muscles, and tendons, especially in the morning.

Breast tenderness.

Headache change. They may increase or decrease.

Gastrointestinal distress. This can include indigestion, flatulence, gas pain, nausea, and sudden bouts of bloat.

Exacerbation of existing conditions. Things you have already seem to get worse.

Increase in allergies.

Weight gain. On average, women may experience a gain of approximately 10 to 15 pounds in the years surrounding menopause, especially around the waist and thigh.

Hair loss. Thinning hair on the head or the whole body is usually temporary in women and rarely of concern. An increase in facial hair is also usually slight and controllable by tweezing.

Dizziness. Light-headedness or episodes of loss of balance can occur.

Changes in body odor.

Electric shock. Sensation under the skin and in the head can sometimes be felt.

Tingling in the extremities. This can also be a symptom of B_{12} deficiency or diabetes. The tingling can result from an alteration in the flexibility of blood vessels in the extremities.

Gum problems, increased bleeding, burning tongue.

Brittle fingernails. Fingernails may peel and break easily.

Depression. Yeah, because this list is so long!

A New Attitude

Call it mental-pause or a menopausal moment. Women at midlife finally have their act together—we just forgot where we put it. Jill Briscoe recalls a scene at a grand opening of a new hospital. She was a guest of honor and sitting on the front row when one of the patients of the Alzheimer wing came up to her and began asking her some unusual questions. Thinking the patient might be confusing her with a member of the hospital staff, Jill said to the elderly woman, "I'm afraid I am not who you think I am. Do you know who I am?" To which the sweet woman replied, "Well...no, dear, but if you go to the front desk they will tell you."

I do want to grow older graciously. I want to think I'd be as encouraging as this e-mail greeting my mother sent me:

> May your hair, your teeth, your face-lift, your abs, and your stocks not fall; and may your blood pressure, your triglycerides, your cholesterol, your white blood count, and your mortgage interest not rise.

> May you receive a clean bill of health from your dentist, your cardiologist, your gastroenterologist, your urologist, your proctologist, your podiatrist, your psychiatrist, your plumber, and the IRS.

> May you find yourself seated around the dinner table with your beloved family and cherished friends.

> May what you see in the mirror delight you, and what others see in you delight them.

HRT or No HRT, That Is the Question

Nothing is more personal or controversial about menopause than hormone replacement therapy (HRT). HRT is a program of estrogen and progestin that is administered to relieve peri-menopausal and menopausal symptoms. It can lower the risk of osteoporosis, colorectal cancer, and perhaps Alzheimer's. After menopause, HRT can also relieve the thinning and drying of your vagina. From 1950 to 1970, doctors routinely prescribed estrogen, and then they noticed a rise of endometrial cancer in women taking estrogen. They added progestin and noticed the risk dropping. Low levels of estrogen place you at risk for osteoporosis, hardening of the arteries, heart disease, increased risk of some cancer, and memory changes. Preventing these situations, plus relief from things such as hot flashes, insomnia, other menopausal frustrations, and a boost to the libido, are why most women seek out HRT.

Choosing whether to pursue HRT is not a simple decision. The list of the pros and cons can make your head swim. For example, in one study, the group gaining the most help after the menopause were those on hormone replacement therapy. Half those on HRT reported improvements in their sex lives, compared with 18 percent of those not taking the therapy. Two-thirds of those on HRT said their ability to continue to work and pursue a career had improved since menopause, compared with 56 percent of those not on HRT. And 71 percent on HRT reported improvements in overall health and well-being, compared with 48 percent of those not on HRT. The report said women taking HRT were mainly middle class, educated, and well informed. They were "a new elite, nicknamed HRHs, hormone-rich and happy."[2]

On the other hand, in *Menopause for Dummies,* doctors penned this warning, "Women with a history of breast cancer should not take HRT…also women shouldn't take HRT to prevent coronary artery disease or reduce the risk of heart attack according to the recent Women's Health Initiative Study. Women with heart disease, diabetes, high blood pressure, high triglycerides, fibromyalgia, or depression aren't good candidates either."[3] In *Your Perfectly Pampered Menopause,* a summary of HRT risk is given, as those using it have 26 percent more risk of breast cancer, 20 percent higher risk for heart attack, 41 percent higher risk of stroke, 100 percent more risk for blood clots in the lungs, 50 percent greater risk of incontinence, and possible protection from colon cancer, bone fractures, and help with hot flashes, night sweats, insomnia, and mood swings.[4]

However, here's an interesting tidbit of information: One group of women is twice as likely to use HRT—women doctors![5]

Alternatives to HRT

Drs. Mark and Angela Stengler, in their book *Your Menopause, Your Menotype,* give more natural alternatives to HRT. Mark and Angela write: "It really comes down to individualized treatment. You need what is best for you and your situation—and to discover that, you need to note your own symptoms and discover your menotype, be open to different therapies, and see how you respond to those therapies."[6]

I appreciate having information on all the alternatives and options to handle the menopausal and perimenopasual symptoms. I also appreciate knowing what is really going to go into my body. "Some women continue to wonder about the safety and effectiveness of a therapy that replaces the body's natural hormones with extracts of hormones from farm animals...Premarin®, the most widely prescribed hormone in the world, comes from horse urine. Is it any wonder that one of my patients recently asked, incredulously, 'Can that really be *good* for me?'"[7] To get a good handle on your options, Drs. Stengler recommend testing:

- FSH—pituitary hormone level is elevated at the time of menopause

- CBC—complete blood count to look for anemia and to make sure immune cells are normal

- Chemistry profile—this looks at many things including glucose, electrolytes, and liver enzymes

- Thyroid panel (include TSH and free T3)—evaluates thyroid function

- Cardiovascular profile—should include counts for total cholesterol, HDL, LDL, triglicerides, apolipoprotien A1, apolipoprotein B, homocysteine, fibrinogen, lipoprotein A (Lp(a)), C-reactive protein, ferritin, and insulin

- Saliva hormone testing—should include estrone, estra-diol, estriol, progesterone, testosterone, DHEA

- X ray and DEXA (bone density)

What I appreciated most about *Your Menopause, Your Menotype* is the doctors' holistic approach to health in using more natural options, such as progesterone cream, herbs, particular diet additions or extractions, certain vitamins, or specific exercises, based upon specific test results and symptoms.

Danna Demetre, author of *The Heat Is On,* and I both consult Dr. Mark Stengler for our own health issues. Mark and Danna also produce a radio program to help women live longer and stronger. Below are their top ten recommendations on supplements or natural alternatives to pharmaceuticals that can augment your diet to counteract the particular stressors brought on by aging. Consult your own physician and then consider a trip to your local health food store to see if you can locate a few of these on the shelf.

1. *High-potency vitamin-mineral complex.* Busy lifestyles, poor eating habits, and the diminished quality of our food makes supplementation a necessity in this day and age. The foundation of our program (always secondary to good eating) is a quality vitamin-mineral complex ideally taken in at least two doses for maximum absorption. (Note from Pam: I happen to take Usana Essentials because their designer, a partner of Jonas Salk, who created the Polio vaccine, wanted to create a vitamin supplement that would help rebuild a body on the cellular level. You can learn more about this on my website, www.farrelcommunications.com.)

2. *Super green foods.* Super green foods, such as wheat grass, barley grass, alfalfa, chlorella, and kelp, are excellent sources of real foods that enhance our health in multiple ways, including detoxification, increased immune function, blood sugar stabilization, and increased energy.

Despite their plant base, super green foods are an excellent source of protein that is highly bio-available.

3. *Essential fatty acids.* Want to have a sharp mind *and* great skin? The essential fatty acids, omegas-3, -6, and -9, are nutrients you need on a daily basis. Limited food sources for the most lacking "EFA," omega-3, include salmon, walnuts, and flaxseed. Since it is unrealistic for most people to get adequate amounts in their diets, supplementation is essential. It is also important to note that most of us are getting too much omega-6 because of the ingestion of so many vegetable oils. Olive oil is high in omega-9 and should be used as much as possible to counteract this imbalance, which increases the inflammatory response throughout the body.

4. *Vitamin C.* While most animals can manufacture their own vitamin C, humans need to get it in their diet. A potent antioxidant with great immunity-boosting effects, vitamin C also has some of its own unique characteristics. For example, vitamin C is required for the production of collagen, it strengthens capillaries, and it may be helpful for those who bruise easily. It is also very helpful in dealing with arthritis because of its anti-inflammatory properties. As a cancer-fighting agent, vitamin C protects the genetic material in cells (DNA) from damage. The average person can take at least 2000 milligrams per day in divided doses.

5. *Garlic.* This is one of the most researched herbs in the world with extraordinary attributes both as a food and supplement. Its main medicinal benefits include cardiovascular protection, improved cholesterol levels, lowered blood pressure, diminished blood clotting, improved circulation, and protection against cancer and infectious diseases.

6. *Calcium and magnesium.* Calcium is required by every cell of your body for a variety of actions, including muscle contraction, healthy nerves, cell division, and the release

of neurotransmitters that scoot between nerve cells, not to mention healthy bones and teeth. Only ten percent of adults get enough calcium each day. Caffeine, alcohol, and sugar all promote urinary excretion of calcium. Hormone imbalances and poor digestive function can also contribute to calcium deficiency. From 8 years old to 80, most people need at least 1000 mg a day of good-quality calcium, which is best absorbed in 500 mg doses with at least 250 mg of magnesium.

7. *Vitamin E.* Vitamin E is found in the fats of most vegetables and grains. Unfortunately, processing foods destroys this vital nutrient that has both antioxidant properties as well as important support to the nervous system, muscle function, and overall healing. People with diseases such as diabetes, Parkinson's disease, fibrocystic breast syndrome, and multiple sclerosis should have extra E supplementation. The average adult should take 400 IU daily.

8. *Ginko biloba.* This mighty little plant treats a wide range of conditions—from memory impairment and dizziness to headaches and depression. It has an extraordinary ability to increase circulation to the brain and extremities. Its natural blood-thinning effects are important to the prevention of strokes and heart attacks. Suggested amounts are 60 milligrams two to four times per day. For severe cases, like early stage Alzheimer's disease, take 240 to 360 milligrams daily.

9. *Green tea.* With about half the amount of caffeine as coffee, green tea provides a reasonable energy boost without the sharp "ups and downs" of coffee and its calcium-robbing effects. It is a great antioxidant and anticancer agent that also helps the liver with detoxification, which is essential for balancing hormones and cleansing the body of many forms of toxins. Preliminary research shows that green tea can help stabilize blood

sugar and thus indirectly promote weight loss by preventing insulin spikes. Green tea extract is available in liquid and capsule forms.

10. *Milk thistle.* Most people in America have significant toxins in their bodies, and their livers are overburdened. Our bodies are not equipped to deal with the staggering amount of chemicals that bombard us on a daily basis. Milk thistle is a potent herb that works specifically in the protection and revitalization of our liver. It also stimulates good digestion of fats as well as improves elimination. Recommended amounts are one 250 milligram capsule three times a day.

These are just general recommendations. To create a set of supplements that are personalized to your own specific health issues and needs, take a salvia test given by a naturopathic physician. These are medical doctors who have additional training and believe in more natural options to treat health issues. It isn't an either/or approach people should take toward their own health care (either naturopath or traditional MD). Rather, both can be wise choices to gain a full and comprehensive evaluation of your health. If you have a difficult time locating a doctor who does salvia testing, Life Wellness Pharmacy offers in-home tests you can take and mail in (lifewellness.com). I have used them in the past, and they offer personalized consultations after the results are in. A qualified medical expert will give you specific recommendations you can then choose whether or not to follow up on.

Baby Those Breasts!

Professionals in the field encourage women to do three things after 40 to be proactive in the personal fight against breast cancer:

1. Have a regular checkup by an ob-gyn

2. Have a yearly mammogram

3. Do a monthly self-exam

You probably have this hanging in your shower on a card from the American Cancer society (GREAT!). But just in case, in your menopausal moment you lost it or have forgotten to do it each month, here it is again.

The Five Steps of a Breast Self-Exam

Step 1. Begin by looking at your breasts in the mirror with your shoulders straight and your arms on your hips. Look for: breasts that are their usual size, shape, and color. Breasts that are evenly shaped without visible distortion or swelling.

If you see any of the following changes, bring them to your doctor's attention:

- dimpling, puckering, or bulging of the skin
- a nipple that has changed position or an inverted nipple (pushed inward instead of sticking out)
- redness, soreness, rash, or swelling

Step 2. Raise your arms and look for the same changes.

Step 3. While you're at the mirror, gently squeeze each nipple between your finger and thumb and check for nipple discharge (this could be a milky or yellow fluid or blood).

Step 4. Next, feel your breasts while lying down, using your right hand to feel your left breast and then your left hand to feel your right breast. Use a firm, smooth touch with the first few fingers of your hand, keeping the fingers flat and together.

Cover the entire breast from top to bottom, side to side— from your collarbone to the top of your abdomen, and from your armpit to your cleavage.

Follow a pattern to be sure that you cover the whole breast. You can begin at the nipple, moving in larger and larger circles until you reach the outer edge of the breast.

You can also move your fingers up and down vertically, in rows, as if you were mowing a lawn. Be sure to feel all the breast tissue: just beneath your skin with a soft touch and down deeper with a firmer touch. Begin examining each area with a very soft touch, and then increase pressure so that you can feel the deeper tissue, down to your ribcage.

Step 5. Finally, feel your breasts while you are standing or sitting. Many women find that the easiest way to feel their breasts is when their skin is wet and slippery, so they like to do this step in the shower. Cover your entire breast, using the same hand movements described in Step 4.[8]

There is also a wonderful interactive video explanation on the Susan Komen site at www.komen.org.

Make Friends with the Mammogram

All kinds of jokes are out there on how to prepare for the mammogram (and I included a few to lighten the mood of this chapter). So here's how to prepare for a this life-saving test:

Exercise 1. Open your refrigerator door and insert one breast between the door and the main box. Have one of your strongest friends slam the door shut as hard as possible and lean on the door for good measure. Hold that position for five seconds. Repeat again in case the first time wasn't effective enough.

Exercise 2. Visit your garage at 3 AM when the temperature of the cement floor is just perfect. Take off all your clothes and lie comfortably on the floor with one breast wedged under the rear tire of the car. Ask a friend to slowly back the car up until your breast is sufficiently flattened and chilled. Turn over and repeat for the other breast.

Exercise 3. Freeze two metal bookends overnight. Strip

to the waist. Invite a stranger into the room. Press the bookends against one of your breasts. Smash the bookends together as hard as you can. Set an appointment with the stranger to meet next year and do it again.

Exercise 4. Locate a pasta maker or old wringer washer. Feed the breast into the machine and start cranking. Repeat twice daily.

You are now properly prepared. Okay, those were obviously a joke, but in all seriousness, because like them or not, mammograms help save lives!

What your doctor is looking for in a mammogram are:

Calcifications. Tiny flecks of calcium—like grains of sand—can sometimes indicate the presence of early cancer.

Cysts. Finding a cyst can actually be good news, as unlike cancerous tumors, which are solid, cysts are fluid-filled masses and are very common—and rarely associated with cancer. An ultrasound is the best way to tell a cyst from a cancer because sound waves pass right through a liquid-filled cyst. Solid lumps, on the other hand, bounce the waves right back to the film.

Fibro adenomas. Fibro adenomas are movable, solid, rounded lumps made up of normal breast cells. They are not cancerous, are very common—but these lumps may grow—and any solid lump that's getting bigger is usually removed to make sure that it's not a cancer. At least one radiologist and a doctor will read your results. If any abnormality is found, they will most likely retest, and you can always ask for a second opinion as well.

To find a reputable, reliable technician, ask your ob-gyn or contact the National Cancer Institute (800-4-CANCER) or the American College of Radiology (800-227-5463). For a free mammogram (for women in financial need with no insurance) call 800-4-CANCER (800-422-6237).

If you have questions about tests, biopsies, etc., ask your doctor. Ask what the test will do and when you can anticipate the results. Keep records of all tests and their results. Keep your hopes up. Most of the time there is nothing to worry about, and fretting and stewing won't change the outcome anyway. I love the quote, "Worry is a lot like a rocking chair. It is something to do, but it won't get you anyplace." Function in faith. Go about life as if the outcome will be good news.

Reward Yourself

But because mammograms are stressful, I always try to reward myself after the procedure with some fun shopping, lunch with a friend, or a peaceful walk by the beach. But nothing gives peace like a good laugh. Award-winning humorist Leigh Anne Jasheway-Bryant captures the attitude needed for a successful mammogram:

The First Time's Always the Worst

The first mammogram is the worst. Especially when the machine catches on fire.

That's what happened to me. The technician, Gail, positioned me exactly as she wanted me (think a really complicated game of Twister—right hand on the blue, left shoulder on the yellow, right breast as far away as humanly possible from the rest of your body). Then she clamped the machine down so tight I think my breast actually turned inside out. I'm pretty sure Victoria's Secret doesn't have a bra for that.

Suddenly, there was a loud popping noise. I looked down at my right breast to make sure it hadn't exploded. Nope, it was still flat as a pancake and still attached to my body.

"Oh, no!" Gail said loudly. These are, perhaps, the words you least want to hear from any health professional. Suddenly, she came flying past me, her lab coat whipping behind her, on her way out the door. She yelled over her shoulder, "The machine's on fire. I'm going to get help!"

OK, I was wrong. "The machine's on fire" are the worst words you can hear from a health professional. Especially if you're all alone and semi-permanently attached to A MACHINE and don't know if it's THE MACHINE in question.

I struggled for a few seconds trying to get free, but even Houdini couldn't have escaped. I decided to go to plan B: yelling at the top of my lung (the one that was still working).

I hadn't seen anything on fire, so my panic hadn't quite reached epic proportions. But then I started to smell smoke coming from behind the partition. *This is ridiculous,* I thought. *I can't die like this. What would they put in my obituary? Cause of death: breast entrapment?*

I may have inhaled some fumes because I started to hallucinate. An imaginary fireman rushed in with a fire hose and a hatchet. "Howdy, ma'am," he said. "What's happened here?" he asked, averting his eyes.

"My breasts were too hot for the machine," I quipped, as my imaginary fireman ran out of the room again. "This is gonna take the Jaws of Life!" In reality, Gail returned with a fire extinguisher and put out the fire.

She gave me a big smile and released me from the machine. "Sorry! That's the first time that's ever happened. Why don't you take a few minutes to relax before we finish up?"

I think that's what she said. I was running across the parking lot in my backless paper gown at the time. After I'd relaxed for a few years, I figured I might go back. But I was bringing my own fire extinguisher.[9]

That is a choosin' joy attitude!

Understanding Your Uterus

A lot is going on with those hormones in menopause! So as a result, much can happen to your uterus and all the rest of your vital female organs. Having a Pap smear yearly is wise as you head into the second half of life. Early detection of cancer will increase the chances for successful treatment. At some point, your periods will cease. Until then, you may experience some heavier bleeding. This heavy bleeding typically occurs during the final two to three years before menopause, or during the first few years after the onset of menstruation during puberty. A good rule of thumb to help you determine whether your bleeding is abnormal is: If you are soaking through sanitary protection products and require changing them more than every one or two hours, or having a period that lasts more than seven days, you are probably experiencing heavy menstruation.

Some women are concerned by clots in their menstruation, but clots, in most cases, are a normal part of your menstrual cycle. (The lining of the uterus is shed during menstruation, and any clots you see are part of the uterine lining and, most often, not cause for alarm.)[10] Heavy bleeding can also be caused by fibroid tumors. "It's important to understand that fibroid tumors are usually benign (non-cancerous) tumors that often occur in the uterus of women during their thirties or forties. While the cause of uterine fibroid tumors is unclear, it is clear that they are estrogen-dependent. Several surgical treatments are available for treating fibroid tumors of the uterus including myomectomy, endometrial ablation, uterine artery embalization, and uterine balloon therapy, as well as hysterectomy."[11] (Your physician can explain all the options in detail.) Nonsurgical pharmacological treatments for fibroid tumors are also available. Some women find natural progesterone to be an effective treatment for uterine fibroid tumors. Often, when symptoms are not severe or troublesome, a "wait and see" approach is taken. Once menopause occurs, uterine fibroid tumors typically shrink and eventually disappear without treatment.

There are several types of hysterectomy:

- A *complete* or *total hysterectomy* removes the cervix as well as the uterus. This is the most common type of hysterectomy.

- A *partial* or *subtotal hysterectomy* removes the upper part of the uterus and leaves the cervix in place.

- A *radical hysterectomy* removes the uterus, the cervix, the upper part of the vagina, and supporting tissues. This is done in some cases of cancer.

You can elect to keep your ovaries, which will continue the production of all your hormones, and you will go through menopause on much the same timetable as you would have prior to surgery. If the ovaries are removed in a woman before she reaches menopause, the sudden loss of her main source of female hormones will cause her to suddenly enter menopause (*surgical menopause*). This can cause more severe symptoms than a natural menopause. A hysterectomy is also major surgery and comes with all the risks of major surgery, including the rare risk of death.

Hysterectomy is the second most common major surgery among women in the United States. (The most common major surgery women have is cesarean section delivery.) Each year more than 600,000 hysterectomies are done. About one-third of women in the United States have had a hysterectomy by age 60.[12]

Hysterectomies are done through a cut in the abdomen or through the vagina. The type of surgery that is done depends on the reason for the surgery. Abdominal hysterectomies are more common than vaginal hysterectomies and usually require a longer recovery time. Hysterectomies are most often done for the following reasons: uterine fibroids, endometriosis, uterine prolapse, or cancer. However, cancer affecting the pelvic organs accounts for only about ten percent of all hysterectomies. Some other reasons as to why hysterectomies are done include chronic pelvic pain, heavy bleeding during or between periods, and chronic pelvic inflammatory disease.[13] There are also other treatments for some of the above maladies, so hysterectomy is just one of many options that should be discussed with your doctor.

To Hysterectomy or Not to Hysterectomy?

You may be suffering from continuing, severe problems with pelvic pain and abnormal uterine bleeding. If you have a condition that is not cancer, such as fibroids, endometriosis, or uterine prolapse, your doctor may recommend that other alternatives be tried first before surgery. If you research your alternatives, you will discover recommendations that span the health disciplines, including natural supplements and dietary recommendation, as well as pharmaceuticals (drugs) or less drastic surgical procedures. If these options fail to provide relief, then a hysterectomy may be recommended. One should research hysterectomies extensively because research is mixed on the impact it can have on your life and future. For example, some research says the libido is negatively impacted (usually if the ovaries are also taken), while other studies say a hysterectomy so improves the health of a woman that her libido increases. "Most complications are less serious, and may include reactions to anesthetics, pain, infection, bleeding, and fatigue. Sometimes other pelvic organs such as the bladder and bowel are injured during a hysterectomy. Hysterectomy is also linked to urinary incontinence (problems holding your urine) and loss of ovarian function and early menopause. Some women experience depression and sexual dysfunction after hysterectomy."[14]

If cancer is involved, surgery will most likely be scheduled right away and will be likely viewed as "life-saving." But if it is an elective reason, you can schedule in an eight-week window for surgery and recovery. Women vary on recovery times. I conducted an unofficial survey of every woman I knew or friends of friends who had the procedure to discover what their recovery time was really like and when they felt themselves again. Again, the results of this very unofficial survey of a couple dozen women led me to believe that if the hysterectomy was done vaginally, the recovery time was much less than if it involved a cut into the abdomen. Then the recovery time would resemble the recovery of a C-section, which is usually six to eight weeks.

Most women who had the more major surgery explained that their fitness level going into the surgery had an impact on recovery. The more fit they were, the quicker they bounced back. Also, the more household help they had, and family and friendship support for the practical areas of life, the faster they got well. I got warning after warning telling me that women need to be sure to really rest. Take the entire six weeks, watch movies, rest, and relax. You might think you are feeling better, but if you jump up too soon and pick up your normal work schedule you might relapse. Most women, even those with the more invasive surgery, said they felt themselves again (energy-wise) from between six to eight months after surgery. All of them said they felt great at the one-year anniversary. Most women said they felt dramatically better and were glad they decided on the surgery, but a few regretted the impulsive decision and wished they would have "toughed it out until after their natural menopause." If in doubt, do more research, consult a second opinion, and pray over the choice.

Decision Point

I remember the night I came to a decision point. I had been diagnosed with fibroid tumors years before, and each year they were getting larger. My periods became heavier and heavier and more and more painful. I moved from maxi tampons and maxi pads, to "Instead" (a kind of cup that "caught the flow" and gave me a bit more time between bathroom breaks). But one night, probably my most important speaking engagement to date, I was to keynote before 6000 mothers. My head was throbbing, so I took my migraine medicine. That also helped curb the extreme cramps I was feeling. I went to the restroom five minutes before it was my turn on stage. Huge clots dropped out of me. I put in an "Instead" plus a maxi tampon plus a maxi pad—and I prayed for a miracle. I was to deliver a humorous 20-minute keynote address. And during the last minute of my speech, I could feel the blood running down my leg, soaking my pantyhose. The crowd had no idea what was going on inside me. All I know is I worked harder at that 20-minute speech than I had any before. Praise God, the resulting speech was very well received. The audience was roaring with laughter over my jokes and the place erupted with wild applause on a few occasions even during the speech. It was hard to enjoy the response, however, when I was living in dread fear that any moment I would be standing in a pool of blood! I walked off the stage and straight to the restroom, relieved that I had made it off the stage before the flood happened. That night I decided life was too short to live five minutes from a bathroom, and life was too fun to live in such extreme pain. I didn't know exactly what I was going to choose to do, but I did know I was not going through this ever again. (I'm not going to tell you what I did decide because this decision is between you, God, and the loved ones you choose to involve in the decision.)

Wow, this has been quite the happy chapter, hasn't it? Miserable menopause symptoms, talk of breast cancer, and hysterectomies— that's not quite dinner conversation, is it? But we are good friends, talking over coffee, right? And good friends share information that benefits good friends. Today, grab a girlfriend and have an honest heart-to-heart. Walk on the beach, go for a smoothie (because now you know caffeine is something meno mamas avoid), or simply pull out the Adirondack chairs and soak up some sun (covered with a hat and sunscreen, of course), while you enjoy a few moments of TLC and tea (herbal, that's a given!). Or call up some girlfriends and plan a weekend to do a cancer walk or throw a "Red Dress" party to raise money for protecting women's hearts. Somehow, today, give some tender loving care to a woman in your world.

— Joy Choice —

Chances are you or someone you know is dealing with some symptom of menopause. Create a meno gift basket for yourself or for a friend. Put in some new favorites: a red dress pin (from the American Heart Association), a pink ribbon (or pink ribbon accessory from the Breast Cancer Society), bottled water, a coupon for a smoothie, a handheld fan, a chilled eye mask, a neck roll or "chillow" (a pillow that can go in the fridge for night sweats), moisture rich lotion (for dry skin), some fresh fruit and vegetables (fiber), herbal tea, and, of course, some kind of "FROG" (Fully Rely On God reminder).

Hot Flash Help

Here are a few tips to help you cope with one of the most common menopause issues:

- Dress in thin layers. You can peel off the top layer when a hot flash occurs (without getting arrested!). Drink a glass of cold water or juice at the onset of a flash.

- At night, keep a carafe or thermos of ice water or an ice pack alongside your bed. Many stores sell tubes of cotton material filled with natural substances (usually a grain). You can freeze them and place one around your neck to cool you down or on your forehead if you get a migraine. Buy several so one is always on ice. In a pinch, a bag of frozen vegetables will do.

- Use cotton sheets, sleeping garments, lingerie, and clothing to let your skin breathe.

- Install a ceiling fan. Buy a portable battery-operated mini fan. Or look around for some cute old-fashioned fans. Antique stores have many with darling prints. Keep them on your bedside or in your purse.

Longer and Stronger

*Small steps taken consistently add
up in a big way over time.*

When our Seasoned Sisters group first formed, my friend Maria wrote this poem and brought it in for the "humor section" of our meeting:

Aging Gracefully

*I found a gray hair today, which wouldn't be so bad
Except it makes 51 with the ones I already had.
I have wrinkles on my cheeks and dimples on my thighs,
Moles that sprout a hair or two and bags beneath my eyes.*

*My waist is getting thicker and my teeth aren't quite as white,
So I tell my spouse it's sexier to make love without the light.
I can't remember birthdays or what my kids just said.
It's a miracle that every day I still get out of bed!*

*But I have friends around who love me.
My husband's my best friend.
God has been so good to me and is with me to the end.
My kids have turned out pretty good. I like my mom and dad.
The joyful days outnumber any that are bad.*

*I've learned to be more loving, and when to take a stand,
When to just listen and when to lend a hand.*

I'm thankful for my days on earth, however long they be,
And hope that in many ways I'm aging gracefully.

And when my days are over and I enter heaven's door,
Please, dear God, be full of grace and make me a size four![1]

We're All in This Together!

More of me to love, more of me to lose. Many perimenopausal/
menopausal women find themselves "well rounded." According to
Dr. Theresa Eichenwald, women typically gain one pound a year
from late thirties to mid sixties.[2] I mean, after all, if my body is the
temple of the Holy Spirit, as the Bible declares, then in my early
forties I had a temple expansion project going. I was not eating any
more than I had been eating as a younger woman. In fact, on many
days I was so busy, I was eating much less. (Which was part of the
problem, I discovered later. Skipping meals is a no-no.) But I was
semi-active—not the athlete of earlier—but more active than my
husband, who was losing weight while I was going to the gym and
still gaining. And I discovered I was not alone. There is even a name
for this weird malady of midlife for a woman.

Dr. Harriette Mogul, an endocrinologist from New York Medical
College, was seeing women patients wanting to discuss treatment
for menopause. They were all different ages and races but seemed
to have a common denominator. They were all health-conscious,
nonsmokers, and physically active. Yet they all were complaining
about gaining weight, especially around their midsection, and they
were having a hard time losing their spare tire. They were also complaining of extreme fatigue.

So the good doctor tested blood sugar levels, but at the time of
testing, all the women's levels were normal. However, their blood
pressure was intermittently high, and their blood fats (cholesterol
and triglycerides) were off. Then she gave each woman a test to
measure insulin levels—and the mystery was unfolded. Dr. Mogul
suspected that even though most of the sugar was eventually cleared

from their blood, the elevated insulin level necessary to accomplish this was responsible for the weight gain and fatigue seen in patients with true insulin resistance—a condition marked by both high insulin and high sugar. The medical community now calls it Syndrome X. The symptoms included increased appetite, food cravings, and continued inability to lose weight *despite diet and exercise.*[3] If we have two or more of these symptoms, "insulin resistance with resulting elevated insulin levels, elevated lipids (especially triclycerides); obesity, coronary artery disease, and hypertension,"[4] we likely have Syndrome X. Not surprisingly, all this has also been found to be associated with estrogen deficiency, or menopause.

And consider what our bodies do with carbs. Simple carbohydrates break down faster and thus get into the bloodstream quicker. They turn into glucose, which is either used right away as fuel or stored in cells. The role of insulin is to move the sugar from the bloodstream as quickly as possible and into cells. Once all the cell sites are filled, the body stores the remainder as fat. The excess fatty acids are sent to the liver and turned into cholesterol. In menopause, estrogen and thyroid levels drop while insulin loses its effectiveness in lowering blood sugar, the pancreas works overtime to produce insulin, and more insulin equals more fat, increasing body mass (BM). In short, we gain weight by eating simple sugars (carbs).

Dr. Mogul's (and many other nutritionists' and physicians') solution is a low glycemic diet that helps sugar levels to not spike up and down, which cause weight gain. Larrian Gillespie concurs with much of this assessment of women and food at midlife. Larrian is a graduate of UCLA and practicing urologist and author of *The Menopause Diet,* and she writes of her own menopause experience:

> In my professional experience I had counseled women on hormone replacement therapy but put little emphasis on lifestyle change. Yet I could see that well-disciplined women going through menopause were gaining weight despite eating a "healthy diet." It was enough to make anyone crazy, let alone depressed!

All this had special relevance when it was my figure that began to change as I entered my forties. At first it was gradual, only a few pounds in six months, but within four years I had managed to pack an additional twenty-five pounds onto my petite five-foot-two-inch frame. I became an expert at "dress camouflage," emphasizing my newly developed bust line over my ever expanding waistline, while relegating my "older" clothes to the back of the closet. Large, oversized T-shirts substituted as my new uniform while I filled drawers with belts that were no longer "fashionable" for me. What had once been a dancer's body had now morphed into a spider body—thin arms and legs attached to a large, round torso.

My day of reckoning came when I went in for a physical examination and peeked at my report, which frankly stated: "Forty-five-year-old multiparous white female, mild to moderately obese…" I wanted to scream!!! Me… OBESE!!! I knew what that meant. After all, I had written it about my own patients. Obesity was next to slovenliness, carelessness…a glutton. How dare this man write that about me? Doesn't he understand it is natural to gain weight when you go through menopause?[5]

Larrian explains medically why it is women so easily gain weight.

What I didn't know at the time was the role estrogen played in appetite control. Recent research has implicated estradiol, the most potent and active form of estrogen, in the control of eating. When estradiol levels drop, so does the release of cholecystokinin, a hormone produced by the pancreas which signals our gallbladders to empty. This in turn makes us feel full or satiated, especially when we have any saturated fat in our diet. During menopause, however, women begin to show a substantial delay in gallbladder emptying and just don't feel full as soon as they should. As a result, portion size

increases, and with that the number of calories con-
sumed per feeding.

Changes in our ability to handle carbohydrates add
another wallop. As blood sugar rises, so does our hunger
quotient and any cholecystokinin released not only fails
to signal we're full but, paradoxically, increases our
appetite. So if you are eating a high glycemic carbohydrate...you'll be even hungrier."[6]

To summarize a couple of suitcases worth of research I read on
this issue, the following are diet tips I discovered.

Get a glycemic index. There are many books, often for those with
diabetes, and some "eating plan/diet" books that have this information in them. "The glycemic index (GI) is a numerical system of
measuring how much of a rise in circulating blood sugar a carbohydrate triggers—the higher the number, the greater the blood sugar
response. So a low GI food will cause a small rise, while a high GI
food will trigger a dramatic spike...A GI of 70 or more is high, a
GI of 56 to 69 inclusive is medium, and a GI of 55 or less is low...A
GI value tells you only how rapidly a particular carbohydrate turns
into sugar. It doesn't tell you how much of that carbohydrate is in
a serving of a particular food. You need to know both things to
understand a food's effect on blood sugar. That is where glycemic
load comes in. The carbohydrate in watermelon, for example, has a
high GI. But there isn't a lot of it, so watermelon's glycemic load is
relatively low. A GL of 20 or more is high, a GL of 11 to 19 inclusive
is medium, and a GL of 10 or less is low."[7]

When it comes to a snack, an apple might be 4 or 5 on the index
while a slice of pizza could be 22 or higher. M&M's are 6 while a
Pop-Tart is over 20. Strawberries are a 1, cornflakes are 26. One
free list of foods and their index score is found at: www.mendosa.
com/gilists.htm. This information revolutionized the way I looked
at food. Things I thought were off limits, like some pasta, I actually discovered were less "GI" than, say, something I perceived as

better for me, such as wild rice. (There are great cookbooks that have recipes for low GI too.)

Get easy access to water. You will be drinking a lot of it! Most experts agree that 64 ounces (8 glasses) a day is minimal. But if you are overweight, one 8-ounce glass is recommended for each additional 25 pounds of body weight. "Take your weight and divide it by 2. Drink that many ounces of water each day."[8] Danna Demetre, author of *Scale Down,* recommends: "At the first sign of fatigue, drink a tall glass of water. Better yet, drink 4 to 6 ounces every hour you are awake and even more when you are exercising."[9]

Get some sleep. If you want to feel younger, stronger, and lose weight—get enough sleep. Eve Van Cauter, professor of medicine, University of Chicago, said, "Since the brain is fuelled by glucose, we suspect it seeks simple carbohydrates when distressed by lack of sleep."[10] One study found that the less people slept, the more they weighed.[11] For most women, an eight-hour minimum is wise. To battle insomnia, which is common in menopause, clock out by creating a sleep prep routine. Wind down earlier. Keep the lights low and mellow out in the late evening. Try a book instead of TV. Move your exercise to earlier in the day. Draw a bath, and walk away from the computer, volunteer work, or housework at a set time each evening.

Get some good habits. Eat breakfast! Don't eat dinner close to bedtime (recommended at least three hours before), and if you must snack, make it veggies or, as my doctor says, "something with skin on it" with loads of fiber (apple, orange, etc.). In the Bible we see Daniel asking King Nebuchadnezzar for this kind of diet instead of rich, lavish food. In the end, Daniel saw God's power and His miracles, and he was elevated to second in the kingdom. Now there's a nice plug for fruits and veggies! Carole Lewis of First Place recommends eating in the same place, eating slowly so your stomach knows when you are full, and not eating in front of the TV. I love Carole's views because instead of a diet ("die"-it), the First Place eating program is called the "Live It" plan! Who wants the concept of death anyplace after 40! So get a "live it" plan.

My friend Danna Demetre, a healthy-living expert, has two terrific questions women should ask so they can maintain a more healthy lifestyle:

1. "Am I doing the right things for the right reasons and trusting God with the results?" (The point is not to reach a weight on the scale or a specific size, but rather take great care of the body God has given you.)

2. "Can I eat and exercise this way most days for the rest of my life?" If the answer is no, then you've just gone on another diet or "program." If the answer is yes, you've made a lifestyle change, and there is a greater chance that the results will be lasting. You need to lose weight the same way you plan to keep it off—and that must be through a lifestyle change.

Get some fiber in you. You can take fiber as a supplement or simply choose foods with a higher fiber content. Whole grains, fresh fruits, and vegetables are great examples. Many breakfast cereals claim high fiber content. Find one that is also low GI, and this may be a simple way to get daily fiber. You can also buy a fiber supplement in powder form and simply mix it into beverages, sauces, and casseroles.

Get used to protein. Protein will keep your blood sugar from spiking (and that is the major cause of the weight gain in life's second half). Just watch portion size on this (and everything else). A portion of protein (such as meat), is usually no bigger than the size of your fist (or the size of your palm). You'll want to skip highly salted or preserved meats in favor of more lean cuts of chicken and fish.

Get a plan to "graze." Small meals closer together will also keep your sugar level from spiking. Snacking on mini snacks of 250 calories can keep your insulin levels down and lower cholesterol. The closer the meals, the lower the glucose and the less insulin levels are, so plan on eating something every few hours. When you graze, try to select low calorie options. Colette Bouchez, in *Your Perfectly*

Pampered Menopause, says, "If you reduce your caloric intake by just 300 to 400 calories daily, you will generally compensate for the slowdown in your midlife metabolism."[12]

Get motivated. For me, one of the most freeing things I did when I really began to take my own health and wellness seriously in life's second half was I did a "cleanse." Usana has a five-day cleanse that is similar to an adapted fast, but it "resets" your body. I took this time to select verses to pray over my life and family, exercise instead of eating my regular meals, and work the program of protein and fiber components that "cleanse" your digestive track yet still provide energy. I played praise music behind my life, listened to the entire Bible on CD that week, and basically took time to *focus forward* by fasting from life in the normal rhythm. It broke my addiction to simple sugars/carbs, and it also gave God an opportunity to speak into my life. This book, Seasoned Sisters as an organization, and other positive changes were the result of that weeklong fast. You might also decide to do a more traditional fast from solid foods and drink just juices, clear broth, or water. Before any fast, consult your physician.

Hold Up Your Heart

We women are very aware of the breast cancer campaign each time we see their pink ribbon. However, what we should be even more concerned about is heart attack. The Red Dress campaign, sponsored by the American Heart Association, is a campaign in high gear trying to get the message out that heart disease is the number 1 killer of American women. In fact, one in three women dies of heart disease. Unfortunately, most women don't know the "Heart Truth." "In 2005, only 20 percent of women identify heart disease as the greatest health problem facing women today."[13] Two years later, because of the Red Dress campaign, 55 percent of women know that heart disease is women's biggest risk in life. Women are ten times more likely to die from heart disease than from any other disease.[14]

What does a heart attack feel like in a woman? It is possible for a heart attack in a woman to have symptoms like back pain, bloating, chest pain even when resting, fatigue, heartburn or pain in the abdomen, jaw or joint pain, lightheadedness, fainting, shortness of breath, pallor, anxiety, and sweating. So a heart attack may not even feel like a heart attack to a woman. It may even feel like a bad case of the flu! You are at risk if there is a family history, you have a high BP, elevated LDL and low HDL cholesterol, diabetes, smoke, eat more than 50 grams of fat a day and are overweight, and if you are not exercising for cardio care.

Sugar That Isn't So Sweet

More than 16 million people in the U.S. have diabetes. The American Association of Diabetes says another 5 million are walking around with it but are unaware that they have it. Eighty percent of people with diabetes are obese, (twenty percent over their ideal body weight). Some symptoms that could indicate you are susceptible to diabetes are: overweight, extreme thirst, frequent urination, constant hunger, fatigue, itchy skin or genitals, pain or numbness in extremities, or slow healing wounds. If you lose weight through exercise and eating well, you can turn back the clock on your risk for diabetes. The more overweight you are, the greater your risk for diabetes, and even a small amount of weight loss will lower your risk. "Postmenopausal women who exercise regularly are about half as likely to develop diabetes as their more sedentary counterparts." [15]

All Stressed-Out and Nowhere to Go

Hypertension (high blood pressure) is diagnosed when a patient's blood is pushing too hard against the walls of the arteries. High blood pressure can lead to life-threatening disorders in the kidneys, blindness, heart disease, and stroke. Since we've talked about heart disease, the other set of symptoms you should be aware of are those of a stroke. A stroke may begin with slurred speech or difficulty understanding speech, dizziness, vision loss, numbness or weakness in an arm, leg, or one side of the body. If someone is acting "off" (not themselves) and you know they have blood pressure issues, do the "STR" test: ask her to *smile,* ask her to *talk,* ask her to *raise both arms.* If she can't do this, rush her to the hospital.

Blood pressure is recorded as two numbers—the systolic pressure (as the heart beats) over the diastolic pressure (as the heart relaxes between beats). The measurement is written one above or before the other, with the systolic number on top and the diastolic number on the bottom. Normal blood pressure is less than 120 systolic and less than 80 diastolic. A blood pressure level of 140/90 or higher is considered high. Those in midlife face a 90 percent chance of developing high blood pressure sometime during their lives. And like many medical issues, your risk goes up if there is a family history of high blood pressure. About one in three adults have hypertension, and many more have it but are unaware. This is why it has been called a "silent killer."

Things that lower blood pressure are:

- physical activity
- a healthy eating plan that emphasizes fruits, vegetables, and low-fat dairy foods
- choosing and preparing foods with less salt
- alcohol in moderation
- little or no caffeine

Have you heard that a glass of wine a good for your health? This suggestion is a bit controversial. Some studies say a glass of red wine a day might be helpful. Other menopause experts say never drink alcohol. I, myself, am a nondrinker, but you do the research (medically and biblically) and decide before God what is your best overall choice. Some experts recommend pomegranate juice as a nice alternative beverage for the health conscious.

You'll want to cut out fast food, table salt, and salty foods first.

Read labels because salt is in much of what sits on the grocery store shelves (most anything in a can or jar or box). Try to lower your daily sodium intake to 1500 milligrams per day.[16] In addition, you may want to add in potassium, magnesium, and calcium to your diet.

Finally, making lifestyle changes to get more sleep, renegotiating responsibilities to create a more "normal" workload, or solve other stressor issues (get counseling for relationship problems, get some space between you and the person who is driving you crazy at work, etc.) are wise moves too. Ask yourself, "Is this responsibility worth losing my life?"

Oops! Don't Fall

> [Osteoporosis] is a condition characterised by the loss of bone density resulting in fragile bones that are at risk of fracture. A woman's bones generally reach their peak bone mass by her mid-20s, dependent on factors such as genetic disposition (i.e., family history), diet, calcium availability and exercise. After the age of about 35, the natural process of bone reabsorption becomes greater than bone formation, resulting in net bone loss. At menopause, this bone loss is accelerated due to the reduction in oestrogen (thought to play a significant role in slowing down the process of bone reabsorption). The highest bone loss occurs immediately after menopause for 5-10 years.
>
> It may be useful to think of bone mass functioning like a bank. If there is a good initial deposit of bone (peak bone mass), then there will be more bone from which withdrawals (bone loss) can be made. If a woman does not achieve an adequate peak bone mass and/or does not maintain strong bones throughout her life (by eating a calcium-rich diet and participating in vigorous weight-bearing exercise), she is at risk of osteoporosis. Women who think they may be at risk of osteoporosis can have a bone density test.[17]

"Women who incorporate 20–30 minutes of physical activity every day can maintain their present weight..."[18] Wonderful women, sweet seasoned sisters, give yourself permission to play! This week, try one of these ideas that you haven't done for a while:

- Walk, jog, run with a friend, on a trail, around a lake, at the beach, or even on the treadmill in front of the TV.

- Line dance, take dance lessons (ballet, tap, jazz, hula, hip-hop), or enjoy dancing with a partner (tango, salsa, waltz, swing, or square dance).

- Swim or take water aerobics.

- Buy a kayak, kneeboard, wakeboard, or surfboard.

- Take up bowling, tennis, racquetball, or handball.

- Rollerblade or ice-skate.

- Join a team: volleyball, softball, soccer.

- Buy a bike—mountain, multispeed, stationary, or recumbent.

- Begin to kickbox, hit a punching bag, jump rope, play badminton, cross-country ski, snowboard, or join a gym.

Finding Your BMI

To set goals and track your progress toward better health and active living, knowing your body mass index (BMI) is a great help. You can have your BMI calculated for you at The Center for Disease Control website, www.cdc.gov/nccdphp/dnpa/bmi/calc-bmi.htm. Or if you'd like to see where your BMI is on the bell curve of all women: www.halls.md/body-mass-index/bmi.htm. In basic math terms, to figure your BMI, (1) multiply your height in inches by itself, (2) then divide your weight (in pounds) by the number you got from step 1, and (3) multiple this number (from step 2) by 705. If it is under 25, you are in the healthy range. An amount over 25 begins to place you at risk, and over 30 should get your attention as someone who needs to take steps TODAY to live a more healthful life.[19] BABY, YOU ARE WORTH IT! If you are over 30 BMI, you might need some help and encouragement reducing your BMI, so call a health clinic, nutritionist, or doctor's office.

If you have a waist size of more than 35 inches, you are considered to be at especially high risk for health problems. For example, if you carry weight around the middle (shaped like an apple), your risk of breast cancer rises six times as those women who carry their weight in their hips and thighs. Set a new goal for wellness by calculating your ideal weight based on a variety of medical and insurance and health tables, with regard given for your age and gender, at: www.halls.md/ideal-weight/body.htm. Then set up a wellness plan for getting closer to your ideal weight. Even modest weight loss will lower your health risk.

Try First Place or other nutritional programs. Visit a health club, especially one that caters to women, like Curves, to discover places with some encouraging women around you daily to "sister" you to wellness. My friend Danna sisters me each time she says, "Small steps taken consistently over time add up in a big way!" Danna has a unique device called a Caltrac that calculates your calorie intake each day and how many calories you used up in activity. The goal is to use up more than you take in. Danna explains, "Most people underestimate the number of calories they eat and overestimate the number of calories they burn. So why do people mysteriously gain 20 pounds by the time they are 40 or 45 years old? It's the 'tic tac' principle. Simply eating just 10 calories (2 breath mints) more than you burn each day can result in 20 pounds in 20 years! With Caltrac, you KNOW how many calories you're burning."[20]

If you are overweight, my arm is around you in a hug as I say this, "I am in this with you, girlfriend. I also am on the journey to wellness. And I just want you to know you are beautiful, no matter what weight you are! But, sweetie, I know that the people in your world love you, and they want you to be with them a long, long time. You deserve the joy of taking care of yourself so you can live longer and stronger. We need you, girlfriend!" (Hugs!) Your first small step might be to decide what plan to use and ask someone to hold you accountable or "sister" you as you take better care of yourself. There are many sisters who have been where you are; place yourself in their world so you can learn from them.

If you are naturally thin, don't just assume you are healthy. Sometimes genetic issues are a concern, so make sure you have regular checkups for peace of mind.

Know Your Numbers

There are some numbers, some pieces of self-awareness, that you will want to keep track of to best protect your health:

My total cholesterol is: _____ Healthy would be: <200

My HDL is: _____ Healthy would be: >40

(Think "H is for happy, healthy cholesterol" so you want this one to be up, over 40. The easiest way to raise this number is through exercise.)

MY LDL is: _____ Healthy would be: <130

(Think "L is for loser," so I want to lower this one because it is bad.)

Triglycerides are: _____ Healthy would be < 150

Glucose is: _____ Healthy range is: 70-105

My BMI is: _____ Healthy for my age: _____

My weight is: _____ Healthy for me would be: _____

My blood pressure is: _____ Healthy for me would be _____

These are some of the basics, but there are doctors who specialize in even more extensive testing. Often they are naturopathic physicians (www.naturopathic.org) who look for more natural ways to identify and combat family history and other risk issues. Ask your physician if they will do a blood test, salvia samples, or give a comprehensive cardiovascular profile (which gives readings on variables such as HDL2 and HDL3, Lp(a), VLDL1, VLDL2, VLDL3, hs-CRP, homocysteine, fibrinogen), or ask if they have the equipment for a bioimpedance analysis, which will give an accurate readout on things like BMI, lean body mass, basal metabolic rate, hydration, and other base readings that can help you track how healthy your body is getting.[21] Some of the extra tests may or may not be covered under your insurance plan, but you might consider them a wise investment of resources as they can help you gain data to make informed decisions about your health care and wellness plan.

Nevertheless, at the minimum, the information in the section above should *always* be a part of your yearly physical, so make sure to ask for these numbers from your physician. Even tracking these basic health calculations will give you the basic information necessary in monitoring obvious risk factors. If you begin with the obvious, you will be creating movement toward better health, and movement is always good!

So keep your joy and perspective as you revamp and remodel your life. Author Suzanne Levine writes, "Imagine how many good laughs we would miss if our bodies weren't giving us so much hilarious material!"[22]

~ Joy Choice ~

Get a plan! Buy a book to help you make wiser eating choices; make an appointment with a nutritionist, doctor, or take a salvia test; join a weight loss or "lifestyle" program. Then call up a girlfriend and share your goal and ask her to "sister" you to the winner's circle!

What Others Are Saying About Life After 40

- "Your laugh lines turn to wrinkles, the dimples in your knees and elbows fill in, you need glasses to read billboards…and when you at last figure your teenagers are old enough to be told about sex, you've forgotten what it is you weren't supposed to tell them until they were old enough to be told."—Erma Bombeck

- "Middle age: when you're sitting at home on Saturday night and the telephone rings and you hope it isn't for you."—Ogden Nash

- "The wages of a chocolate sundae at sixteen is only the price listed on the menu. But a sundae at forty-five is a double chin and a spare tire around the waist."—Constance Foster

- "People who hide their age, that's sick. I'm very happy to be 42. I can't wait to be 55. I'm gonna be an awesome diva by then."—Patti LaBelle

- "When you reach 40, you may still have a fear of pain, but you also have the knowledge that you'll survive it."—Mariette Hartley[23]

Love Lavishly

Now faith, hope, love, abide these three;
but the greatest of these is love.

⟨⟩

I unwrapped the gift the leadership team had given me for speaking. Three lovely boxes, tied with golden ribbon. Out of the boxes came three angels. They were fun, folksy, and fantastic reminders to me of all that it takes to make relationships work. Their names were etched into ribbons they held: *Faith, Hope,* and *Love.*

Bill and I spend the majority of our time helping people make relationships work. We have numerous books for married couples: *Men Are Like Waffles—Women Are Like Spaghetti; Love, Honor and Forgive; Every Marriage Is a Fixer-Upper;* and *Red-Hot Monogamy.* We also speak to singles in our book *Single Men Are Like Waffles—Single Women Are Like Spaghetti.* Some think that teaching people relationship skills requires a slant for married couples and a slant for singles, but I don't think that type of separation will capture the entire spectrum of what is important after 40. Love is love, no matter what state of life you find yourself in. Married or single, we are all commanded to love.

Jesus said, "By this all men will know that you are My disciples, if you have *love* for one another" (John 13:35). The Bible tells us what love looks like in 1 Corinthians 13:4-8:

> Love is patient, love is kind and is not jealous; love does not brag and is not arrogant, does not act unbecomingly; it does not seek its own, is not provoked, does not

take into account a wrong suffered, does not rejoice in unrighteousness, but rejoices with the truth; bears all things, believes all things, hopes all things, endures all things. Love never fails.

Love is seamless. Whether we are single or married, love is the trait that produces influence and draws people into our hearts and lives. Girlfriend, it is certainly in your best interest to decorate your life with love because your relationship state could change very quickly. If you are single, Mr. Right might enter your life any day. There is no expiration date on the institution of marriage. If you are married, chances are (according to statistics), you will outlive your husband and find yourself flying solo once again. Forty-three percent of the population in the 2004 census described themselves as single.[1] Fifty-three million had never been married, and 22 million were currently divorced, while 14 million were widowed.[2] The Bible actually calls us to "be *content* in whatever circumstances" we find ourselves (Philippians 4:11) because God has a plan for each of us at every age and stage of life. The key to making it happen is to let love flow. Love is what makes us attractive, winsome, and magnetic. Love draws people to us. Love makes you "that girl."

"That Girl"

You have to know "that girl." Maybe *you* are "that girl." She is the one about whom people say:

- She's so nice.
- She's so together.
- She has it all going on.
- She always has a following.
- She's so gracious.
- She's so classy.
- She's elegant.

- She's so energetic and enthusiastic.

- She's so sweet.

- She has something I want.

Girl, you can have "it!" because the "it" is love. Women who know how to love lavishly, heartily, fervently, faithfully, and art-fully are women people want to be around. Some of us are called to be married and apply love there, while others are called to be single and share love through other venues, but we are all called to love.

Being a loving person isn't always easy, is it? Maybe you've found yourself praying something like this recently:

Dear Lord,
I pray for Wisdom to understand my man;
Love to forgive him;
And Patience for his moods.
Because, Lord, if I pray for Strength,
I'll beat him to death. AMEN

So let's take a closer look at love through the eyes of those three angel reminders, Faith, Hope, and Love. They stand guard near my mirror, reminding me as I look in it each day, "Are you being an angel of love?" In the Bible, angels are God's messengers, and although you are not some cherubic creation dwelling in the heav-enlies, you still can be a messenger of God's love here on earth.

Angel of Faith

Women who love lavishly have an ability to see the potential, the positive, and the promise—not the problem. Check out this defi-nition of faith from Hebrews 11:1 in the *Amplified* version of the Bible: "Now faith is the assurance (the confirmation, the title deed) of the things [we] hope for, being the proof of things [we] do not see and the conviction of their reality [faith perceiving as real fact what is not revealed to the senses]."

Faith is like a postdated check. We can't get our hands on the money yet but we know one day we will. In the same way, a woman of faith sees the promise as good as reality. Her faith helps her function in the realm of "what can be." Your vision is focused by faith-colored glasses, and those glasses help YOU look better too, my dear!

I interviewed many of my single friends over 40 for this book, but I only interviewed the ones who were POSITIVE. I asked them to describe the upside of single life and together they created a list of more than 50 things! Here are a few of the fun ones:

- You can paint your house or apartment any color you want and decorate any way you please.

- You can be as busy or as lazy as you want within reason.

- Life's an adventure when it comes to figuring out home improvement and repairs. While it would be nice to share many responsibilities with someone else, you learn just what you're capable of. It stretches and grows you in new areas.

- Spontaneity is all up to me, not someone else's schedule.

- I do not have to consult with anyone on how I spend my money or my time.

- I am free to serve God when and how I wish.

- I can have cereal—or even ice cream—for dinner.

- I never have to share the remote!

Peggy Rentz, one of my single "sisters," was so positive she penned a poem that depicts her ability to see the upside of life:

Spinster's Lament

My mama, she panicked because I'm not married.
She said I'm too picky and took me to task.
"But, Mama!" I cried. "How was I to know that
The last man to ask me would be last to ask?

According to Newsweek, *when I have reached 40,*
If I am not married, it's catch-as-catch-can.
Statistically speaking, I've more chance of catching
A terrorist's bullet than catching a man.

I've been educated in schools of high learning.
I'm witty and talented...bright as can be.
Though top of my class, I've yet to accomplish
The one thing I want: an M-R-S degree.

Once over 30 the body starts failing.
I'm over the hill now and hitting the skids.
My plumbing is shot and my memory's fading...
And I just remembered I forgot to have kids!

We are independent, assertive, and ambitious.
We know where we're going and aim for the top.
We don't understand why the men all ignore us,
'Cause Newsweek *says we are the cream of the crop.*[3]

All my single friends are my friends because I love their positive attitude. I love hanging out with them because they see themselves as whole and they see their state of life as a gift. One friend wrote in an e-mail:

> I really had to learn to cling to God when I lost the love of my life. It was the worst thing that ever happened to me emotionally and the best thing that ever happened to me spiritually. It is hard for a...single woman to imagine, but God has so much more for us than we can see. We grasp for what we think we desire without trusting that God has the ability and creativity to give us bigger, better desires...and to fulfill them!

The Midlife Marriage

Those of us who are married also need to be able to grasp the fact that God can fulfill those desires we long for. Some of us are selecting a permanent solution for a temporary problem. Midlife is the number one time for couples to toss in the towel on their marriages. But it isn't just because of men and affairs. The number of women having affairs has risen significantly in recent years, as has the divorce rate for those over 40. More women are bailing out on their marriages at midlife. In the AARP survey of those who divorced from ages 40 to 69, 66 percent of women reported that they asked for the divorce.[4]

The ability to hang on and love is a bit easier when we realize all that is going on in a male's heart and mind in midlife. Years ago, when my oldest (who is now 23) was 3, I went with my husband to pick up his father for a lunch date. While Bill went into the building to get his father, I stayed in the car with my newborn and my toddler. The parking lot was completely empty, so I decided now would be an appropriate time to nurse my infant. A few moments later, a midlife man in a red convertible sports car drove up next to us and parked. He could have parked anywhere—the parking lot was completely empty—but he chose the spot right next to our car. He just sat in his car, listening to his radio.

My impatient toddler hopped out of his car seat and promptly opened his door, swinging it right into the red sports car! I was mortified—and because I was nursing, it took me a moment to place the baby in his car seat and try to capture my toddler. Brock heard my cry and command to get back in the car and—trying to shut the door—he banged the car again. I looked at the red-faced man. He seemed ready to blow his top. I felt in danger for myself and for my sons. I whisked Brock into the car, locked the door, looked at the man, and mouthed an "I'm very sorry." I prayed my husband would return so that we could trade insurance numbers, etc. I felt horrible that my child had harmed his car. They were tiny dings, but I still felt bad. But I was about to feel worse. The man got out of his car and came over to my window and began to beat on it with his fists, swearing and threatening me and my children. I told him through the closed window that my husband would return and make things right, but he got in his car and peeled off in a huff.

I was crying and upset when Bill returned to our car. I recounted the story to Bill and his father—and they were outraged that any grown man would act in such a manner, especially toward a nursing mother and toddler. But now that I am in midlife myself, I have gained new compassion for the man in the red sports car. I am sure he was a frustrated midlife man. That car might have been the only toy he had. He might have sacrificed for others for years, driving used cars and giving up his golf game so his kids could get tennis shoes. Jim Conway, in his book *Men in Midlife Crisis,* said he felt at midlife like a vending machine because people always wanted something from him. I observed what people this last week wanted from my own over-40 husband:

- Give me your car keys.
- Give me your counsel.
- Give me your money.
- Give me your wisdom.
- Give me your connections.
- Give me your time.
- Give me your talent.
- Give me your resources.
- Give me your prayers.
- Give me your muscles.
- Give me your expertise.

Give me, give me, give me—and he gave and gave and gave. Maybe in giving back to our midlife man, we can help lessen the pressure so he won't be the one in the red convertible screaming at helpless women and children.

Who Stole My Husband?

Jeff was a very conservative pastor. You know, poster boy for the

Republican party type. Blue blazer, khaki slacks, and coordinating tie was what he wore into the pulpit each Sunday. That is, until he hit midlife. One day he appeared in a Hawaiian shirt buttoned up halfway, shorts, and Birkenstock sandals. He let his hair grow out until it reached his shoulders. He got his ear pierced and was talking about getting a tattoo. Jeff and his wife, Karen, had eight children but he was talking of selling the family van to get a Harley-Davidson motorcycle. He was playing his favorite rock tunes from high school, such as "Born to Be Wild." Karen said to me, "Who stole my husband and when will they bring him back?"

Karen dug in and learned as much as she could about men and midlife (for much more on midlife for both men and women, see www.midlife.com). She read books, went to seminars, and found a counselor specializing in midlife issues. What she learned was that men at midlife are asking a few key questions:

1. Is this the career I want to work in for the rest of my life?

2. Have I made my mark on the world?

3. I am mortal and I don't like it. How can I feel young again?

4. Why do I feel so lost? (He may have unresolved emotional baggage from his childhood that comes back screaming to be resolved.)

5. I have spent so much time on work, I feel like a stranger in my own family. How can I get closer to my wife and children?

6. I want a deep relationship. Who will listen to my heart? (The wise wife will want this to be her. The wise midlife man will seek ways to get reconnected to his wife.)

Karen went to Sally Conway, a specialist in the area of midlife, for advice. Sally said, "Look at him through the eyes of an 18- or 19-year-old. What traits, what qualities would an 18- or 19-year-old woman find attractive in your husband? You find them attractive too. Your spouse doesn't need another mother right now. He needs you to be his girlfriend."

It will take time to be your husband's girlfriend. He'll need time for you to listen to his heart, to be his sounding board, to be his date and his sexual playmate. One day over lunch, Karen said to me, "Pam, it takes a lot of time to be your husband's girlfriend. I have to shave my legs every day!"

Karen set aside some of her dreams, plans, and responsibilities to be her husband's confidante and lover. She invested in things that made him feel valued—and she encouraged him to get that Harley. Karen said, "It is cheaper than a divorce and less complicated than if he got a girlfriend! He needs a new adventure!"

The result: Jeff decided to keep the family van, he cut his hair, he put back on the blue blazer (at least for Sundays) and he returned to school to finish his doctorate. And Jeff and Karen took a second honeymoon, part of the time on the Harley and part on a cruise. One day Jeff turned to Karen and said, "Honey, I've noticed how much you have set aside for me. I appreciate all the time you have listened and all the sacrifices you have made. I want to do something for you. I know you have wanted to start a national organization to encourage women. I want to help you. Whatever I can do, just name it, sweetie." Jeff is now one of Karen's best cheerleaders on a new adventure in life. Karen saved her marriage, got a teammate for life's second half's adventure, and saved all eight of those children a whole lot of pain—just by choosing to realign her priorities to be her husband's girlfriend.

Angel of Hope

Hope can be hard to nail down. What does hope look like? What does hope act like? What would be a working definition of hope? When I am trying to grasp a big picture principle or wrap my mind around a difficult-to-understand truth, I often will read about it (1) in context of the entire passage of Scripture it is in and (2) look at many translations or paraphrases of the Bible of that same verse.

Galatians 5:5-6 says: "For we through the Spirit, by faith, are waiting for the hope of righteousness. For in Christ Jesus neither circumcision nor uncircumcision means anything, but faith working through love" (NASB).

In The Message, Eugene Petersen interprets these same verses this way: "Meanwhile we expectantly wait for a satisfying relationship with the Spirit. For in Christ, neither our most conscientious religion nor disregard of religion amounts to anything. What matters is something far more interior: faith expressed in love."

Women who love lavishly have a hope that waits expectantly. Hope is the feeling you had as a kid on Christmas Eve, the day before the last day of school, or the morning you went school shopping for that fresh box of crayons and new outfit for the class picture. Hope is excited about life. Hope is enthusiastic. Hope is energetic. Hope throws confetti before the parade begins. Hope sends out the party invitations months before, or sometimes years before, the celebration will be held. Hope holds on and holds out for life's best.

Hope looks for the creative way to keep a promise of love. One of my single friends shared this story:

> When both of my nephews turned ten, I took them on trips from Oregon to Yellowstone National Park. On one of those trips I promised my nephew that we could go fishing because that's what we both like to do. It turns out that we couldn't rent a little fishing boat because the company required two people who were strong enough to pull each other out of the water if someone fell in. I was disappointed, but my nephew was crushed. On impulse I told him I had to go to the ladies' room—and I sneakily went into the boat charter office.
>
> Well, I had chartered a fishing boat for us! I had never chartered a boat before, and it was expensive, but I knew it would cheer up my nephew. The next day just the two of us and the captain of the boat went out on Yellowstone Lake. The captain took us to his special fishing hole, and

we caught so many large cutthroat trout that the captain could hardly keep up!

Flip the Coin Over

In our book *Every Marriage Is a Fixer-Upper,* we interviewed couples who had been happily married for more than 20 years and got their advice on what makes long-lasting love. One of the top ten things was to maintain a positive attitude toward your mate. Studies by John Gottman, a leading researcher in marriage, show that the happiest couples have five positive statements for every one negative statement made. Be aware of this principle in marriage: *The thing you first fell in love with can become a source of irritation over time.* It's like two sides of the same coin. For example, you loved that your fiancé was such a great storyteller, but now that he is your husband, he just seems to go on and on with his same old jokes. Or maybe he was fun and footloose, but now he seems irresponsible or haphazard to you. Instead of focusing on the irritation and criticizing, flip the coin over and compliment that thing you first fell in love with. Love with a dash of hope brings change and adds spark and sizzle to your midlife marriage.

In a letter to "Dear Abby," one pastor shared this story: "I once heard about a woman who was unhappy in her marriage and angry at her husband. When she went to her lawyer to begin divorce proceedings, she asked his advice on what she could do to really hurt her lousy husband. The lawyer thought for a moment and suggested that for the next couple of months, she love him and romance him with every ounce of her being, and once he was happy and fulfilled, serve him with the divorce papers. 'It will rip his heart out,' the lawyer promised.

"The woman followed his advice. Several months later, she returned to the lawyer's office. He handed her the divorce papers to examine before serving them to her husband, and the woman replied, 'I won't be needing them now. We're getting ready to leave on our second honeymoon.'"[5]

Angel of Love

Love is easy to define and hard to live out. But at least God provided a model for us. God the Father sent His sinless Son, Jesus Christ, into the world to pay the ultimate sacrifice to ransom and redeem sinful us. As a result, we can be forgiven of those imperfections (sins) and find a new life, and live eternally in heaven someday with Him. Love is always other-centered. Love chooses to give rather than take. Love is the fuel injected into another's dream. Love seeks to understand, give compassion, guidance, or boundaries—whatever is necessary for the person who is the recipient of love to reach her God-given potential.

Lavish love is like infinity; it just keeps extending all that is good, kind, and true forever, not because a person deserves it, but just because it is right to be loving.

One of the most inspirational examples I know of what complete, unconditional love looks like is conveyed in the story of Carmen. It is the story of a love that encompasses faith, hope, and love. I met Carmen while I was traveling, and she shared her journey with me.

One day, as Carmen entered her home with her arms full of groceries, she heard familiar noises coming from the bedroom. She walked in to see her husband and her best friend in bed together. She didn't know what to do: yell, scream, cry, or choke the living daylights out of them both! She ran out, got into her car, and drove to a quiet place to pray. *Lord, this is unreal. This happens to other people, or on TV, but not to me, not to us. We have five kids. This will devastate them. Plus, I've been an at-home mom—God, my whole world is falling apart! What do You want me to do?*

For days she walked around in shell shock, trying to hear from God. Her husband had not only slept with her best friend, but he continued to be verbally abusive to her, saying things like "I never loved you." "You give the kids all the attention." "You have gained weight so I don't find you attractive." The words stung, so she again took her pain to God. *God, show me what You want me to do. I know I can be free to walk away—he did commit adultery. But I don't want to walk away. I want to fight for my family. Satan has won too much ground already. I want to take back ground! God, I believe You can rescue me from this pain and help me love like You. I believe You can save this marriage, but I don't know what to say or not say. Show me.*

God answered with some radical advice, that not many of us would have the courage to put into action.

Carmen felt God impress upon her, *Keep your focus on his positive traits. He has many flaws but keep your focus on the positive. But most importantly, keep your focus on Me. Lean not on your own understanding; I will direct your paths. And, Carmen, only listen to the truth and only speak My truth.*

So when her husband said, "I never loved you," Carmen held out her hand like a crossing guard holding back traffic and said, "I don't receive that. I don't believe that. I know you, and I know you meant it when you said 'I do' on our wedding day. And more than that, I meant it. I said for better or for worse, and right now it is worse, but I believe it can get better again. So no matter what you say or do, I am going to tell you the truth. I love you. I choose to love you."

Carmen began to prayer walk with a mentor, using the 52 Scripture prayers from the *Wives in Prayer Guide* (www.farrelcom munications.com) and Stormie Omartian's *The Power of a Praying Wife*. Months went by. Then one day her husband walked into the living room, where she was sitting reading her Bible. He got down on his hands and knees. He was shaking and crying as he collapsed and threw his head into Carmen's lap and sobbed. "I am so sorry. Please forgive me. I have been so stupid. No one has ever loved me like you do. I was so afraid you'd leave me, and I couldn't bear that. I saw the pain in my dad when Mom left him, and I vowed I'd never hurt like that, so I did something to hurt you. I wanted to leave before you left me. I am so, so sorry. I know I don't deserve it, but can we please start again?"

And start again they did. That was seven years ago. Today they are happily married and run the marriage ministry of their church.

A Love to Look Forward To

For my twenty-fifth anniversary, I saw a plaque I wanted as a reminder for our marriage. It read, "Come away with me, the best is yet to be." At our twenty-fifth anniversary celebration, our friend and musician Anita Renfroe said, "We're here to celebrate Pam and Bill's red-hot monogamy!" Our whole table looked at us and said, "Your next book!" What they didn't know was Harvest House Publishers had already contracted with us to create a book on the topic of sex and romance that would have hundreds of ideas on how to fan the flame on love for a lifetime—it just needed a title. What a way to begin life's second half!

As you look at the second half of your life through the eyes of faith, hope, and love, what would you like to title Part B of your life journey? When you love lavishly, amazing things are possible.

I like the spirit of anticipation of an older couple who went into their local neighborhood drugstore:

> Jacob, age 92, and Rebecca, age 89, living in Florida, are all excited about their decision to get married. They go for a stroll to discuss the wedding, and on the way they pass a drugstore. Jacob suggests they go in. Jacob addresses the man behind the counter. "Are you the owner?"
>
> The pharmacist answers, "Yes."
>
> Jacob: "We're about to get married. Do you sell heart medication?"
>
> Pharmacist: "Of course we do."
>
> Jacob: "How about medicine for circulation?"
>
> Pharmacist: "All kinds."
>
> Jacob: "Medicine for rheumatism, scoliosis?"
>
> Pharmacist: "Definitely."
>
> Jacob: "How about Viagra?"
>
> Pharmacist: "Of course."

Jacob: "Medicine for memory problems, arthritis, jaundice?"

Pharmacist: "Yes, a large variety. The works."

Jacob: "What about vitamins, sleeping pills, Geritol, antidotes for Parkinson's disease?"

Pharmacist: "Absolutely."

Jacob: "You sell wheelchairs and walkers?"

Pharmacist: "All speeds and sizes."

Jacob: "We'd like to use this store as our bridal registry."[6]

When I was in Arizona speaking, I stayed over to hear my friend Pastor Roger Storms teach on marriage because he and his wife, Nancy, have a delightful love of more than 35 years. The next day, Nancy e-mailed me a precious story from a woman in the congregation:

> **To:** Roger Storms
> **Subject:** Keeping On
>
> Dear Roger,
>
> I know that your messages for these four Sundays are geared to the younger and married people in the church, as well they should be. But I want to tell you a quick story about "old" married people too. Two nights before my husband died, he was standing beside the bed while the nurse was changing it. I was holding him as he was quite wobbly and in pain. All of the sudden he reached down and pinched me on the rear. Very surprised, I quickly looked up at him and he had that smile and twinkle in his eyes. I will always remember the love that showed in his face and have a smile to carry with me forever. If the marriage is right, you can "Keep On" right to the end.[7]

That's the kind of love I want—true till the very end!

~ Joy Choice ~

If a book could be written about what you are looking forward to in life's second half, what would you title it?

Lavish love:

- Looks to the potential, positive, and promise, not the problem (faith)

- Has an ability to wait expectantly (hope)

- Keeps extending all that is good, kind, and true, not because a person deserves it, but just because it is right to do (love)

Which role of "an angel" is easiest for you? Which is hardest? Select one: faith, hope, or love, and think of a creative way to express that action to someone in your world this week. It may or may not change the circumstance, but by loving lavishly over and over, you'll find it is changing you. As you look in the mirror, you'll like the woman looking back at you!

It's All Relatively CALM

By the time your kids are fit to live with—
they are living with someone else!

⟿

Q: How many egomaniacs does it take to screw in a lightbulb?
A: One. The egomaniac holds the light bulb while the rest of the world revolves around him.

Sometimes relationships in life's second half can get a bit complicated. Aging parents, teen children, adult children, and even your spouse can get this "the world revolves around me" syndrome. People forget women over 40 are often experiencing major emotional and physical changes. We've consistently been the strong one, so our friends and family just keep expecting it will always be that way. We've always been there for them, so why should they expect any different? You might find that you are praying "The Menopause Prayer" every day lately:

The Menopause Prayer

God
Grant me the hormones to forget the people I never
liked anyway,
The good fortune to run into the ones I do,
And the eyesight to know the difference.[1]

Dealing with people can sometimes NOT bring out the best in us! In addition to people's basic nature to drift toward selfishness, life circumstances often pile up on us as well, which can raise the stress level even more. Every day seems to present a new maze of decisions, questions, and relationships to negotiate. Here are a few common scenarios:

Sheila feels pulled from all directions. Her college-age son thinks she is too controlling. Her mother, with growing dementia, complains that Sheila doesn't have enough time for her. Sheila's daughter, Teresa, is engaged and there is growing tension over wedding plans. Her soon to be son-in-law seems to like her well enough, but *his* mother...now that's another story. Her dad just keeps saying, "Relax. It will all work out." Her oldest daughter, Trisha, depends on Sheila for child care three days a week. Sheila loves time with her grandchildren, but her views on homework, sweets, and TV time are different than Trisha's. Her own daughter keeps correcting her, even though she is babysitting for free! Her midlife husband complains, "We never do anything fun anymore. How about golf on Saturday?" Sheila screams, "Golf! Who has time for golf? It's like I am giving to everyone and no one appreciates it! Seems I can't please anyone! So maybe I will just go play golf!"

Lori wasn't sure if she could make it one more day with her mom and dad in her house. "I love them, but this is much harder than I thought. I know they need me. Their health is failing, and their money is running out. But how can they be so critical of the way I mother my kids when I am, in a sense, mothering them? You'd think they'd be grateful, not grumbling. I tell myself, 'They are old. Their bodies hurt. They feel displaced and sometimes confused because they are not in their familiar surroundings.' My head knows all that, but my heart is having a hard time loving them when they are so unappreciative. I never understood elder abuse until now. I wonder if it is often an act of self-defense! Did I just say that out loud? Oh my goodness, see what a mess I am?"

Candy said, "I now know why your kids should never move home again after college. Yikes. Everyone tells me, 'Oh, Jenna is such a nice girl! What an incredible person she is—so upwardly mobile.' I wish. She works all the time but thinks I should be her cook, housekeeper, and laundress. We are doing her a favor by letting her move home to save for a down payment on a house. Is it too much to ask that she cook a meal once in a while, pick up after herself, or offer to buy a few groceries? She's making more than I am, so I know she can afford it. I am not her maid!"

In life's second half, we women get an inner desire for calm because often the interpersonal chaos and life's torrential storm of change whips around us like a hurricane. We long for the same feeling we get when lying in a hammock on a beach in Hawaii and having a waiter bring us a cool fruit smoothie. Aaaah! Can't you just feel the soothing island breeze melt away that stress?

Since most of us can't escape to Hawaii on a daily basis, and those who live in Hawaii still have the same issues all the rest of us do around the world, what are some other skills we can use to create the sense of calm we are in search of? In all our years in the people-helping profession, there are a few simple skills we see that, if people master, can help them maintain that inner peace, balance, positive confidence, and a "love of life" attitude we all long for. To make it easy to remember, let's link these skills to the word, CALM.

C are enough to confront

A ccept that people grow and change

L earn to forgive, reconcile, and release

M ove yourself forward

Maintaining calm can be quite a chore, so this acrostic will actually take two chapters to complete. ("I know, I know!" you say. "Some of my relationships have taken hundreds of chapters to get to calm!") Well, we have many issues to cover here. How do we relate to our parents when we have to parent them? How do we handle our grown kids when we can't just send them to their room anymore? (Or can we? Hmm.) How do we manage friendships when we are all so imperfect? And then, how do we adjust to daughters and sons-in-laws, with whom we want to have loving relationships even when we cannot figure them out at all? And then there is the wonderful payoff for working at our relationships—grandchildren!

A friend of mine with a delightful sense of humor was sharing pictures of her three grandchildren with me. I hadn't seen her for some time, so I mentioned to her that I was writing this book and was looking forward to my own chapter as a grandmother someday. She shared that she was a part of her grandchildren's caregiving team, so she regularly saw them twice a week.

"What do they call you?" I asked. "There are so many cute options these days: Nana, Gama, Uma…"

"Oh, all my grandkids greet me with, 'Hello, my beautiful Nana!'"

"That is just precious! How did they come up with that?"

"I taught them. I figure as I get older I want someone to think I am beautiful!"

I like her grandparenting philosophy.

Don't we wish all relationships could be as simple and sweet as the innocence of a new relationship with a grandbaby? But as people grow up, they sometimes get harder to live with. (People might even say that about you and me someday too.) When things get complicated, remember what you are going for is CALM.

Care Enough to Confront

I was away at college when my sixteen-year-old sister called. She had phoned my mother's doctor, a friend of my mom's from Al Anon, and a lawyer. What prompted a very shy teen to make such assertive phone calls while most of her peers were doing after-school sports or watching reruns of *The Brady Bunch?*

Every night Dad would drink himself into an angry, raging frenzy. He would throw things and break things. I was home for spring break that year, and in the middle of the night, he would come into my room and say things like, "I should just die. You'd all be better off without me. Might as well just have my insurance. Life is not worth living. Charlie (my nickname), do you think life is worth living?"

Sometimes he'd have a bottle of pills in his hand, other times a rope, a stick, or bat. Fearful for all of our lives, either my mother or I would try to talk life and sensibility into my dad. Our goal was to keep him alive just one more night with hopes that the next day might be better. We kept believing he would be willing to contact a professional to help him make his way back to sobriety and sanity. But that day never came. In fact, one night my mom, my brother, my sister, and I locked our bedroom doors because we feared we might be tomorrow's headline: "Man kills wife, children, himself."

During the day we'd all try to talk Dad into joining Alcoholics Anonymous (AA) for the zillionth time, only to relive the insanity over again each night. After Easter break, my eternally optimistic mom talked me into going back to college. I wanted to believe she was right when she said, "I can handle it, sweetie," but I worried about her and my siblings. Each time I came home, my frail mother was thinner, more gaunt, and more worn looking. The sleepless nights filled with the vigilant attempt to keep my dad from killing himself, her, or the kids was wearing on her soul.

It finally came to a breaking point the night before I received that phone call from my little sister, Deney. When Deney left for school, our mother was sitting in the shower, scrubbing tile grout. Six hours later, Deney walked into the house to find Mom still sitting in the shower, scrubbing tile grout with a toothbrush, and crying. She'd been in there all day. The night before, the chaos in the home had escalated. In retrospect, 911 should have been called, but all of us had become accustomed to the turmoil of my father's drinking. We had become numb to our own pain, especially my brave mother, who loved unconditionally, no matter what Dad did or said. What she didn't realize then, but quotes now, is that she was living out the definition of insanity: doing the same thing over and over again and expecting a different result.

That day, sitting in a shower with a toothbrush, Mom's heart and spirit broke. She couldn't take it one more day, even one more minute. My mom was a shell of her former self. I don't remember which of us called my grandmother, three states away, but she came, seemingly overnight, to rescue her daughter. My grandparents would have come sooner, but we were all so convincing when we'd say, "I'll be okay, really."

Mom wasn't okay, so we took her to her physician. I am not sure of the exact medical term—mental breakdown, emotional trauma, or battered wife syndrome—but my mom had it. She was so exhausted and depressed that getting dressed was a major accomplishment. The doctor dished out some strong but life-saving advice.

"As I see it, you have three choices: One, you can stay and one of two things will happen. He will kill you and maybe the kids too, or you'll snap and you'll kill him. Two, you will become so depressed you will die of self-neglect or suicide. Three, you and the kids can get out and give him an ultimatum to get help. Maybe he can re-earn the right to be in all your lives, and if he really gets serious, this track might save the marriage and family system."

Sobering words. Saving words. Words that became the lifeline of hope and help to a family drowning in pain. My mom was 40. This was not a great way to start the second half of life. Supported by myself, my siblings, and my grandmother, Mom calmly explained to Dad, "I love you. We all love you, but we can't live like this anymore. I have asked you to get help. We have begged you to go to AA. We know God can help you, can help us, find a better way to live. Until you go into treatment, it just isn't safe for me and the kids here anymore, so we are leaving. I will be at my mother's. After you get help, call me. Then we'll see what the future might hold. Right now, we have to leave."

So we left. My father was brokenhearted and sad, but unrepentant. In denial, he helped pack the U-Haul, trying to convince all of us that the problem was Mom, not his drinking. I remember telling him, "Daddy, why do you love the bottle more than us? Just call the doctor and go into treatment. Show us that you love us more."

We piled into the moving van, and I sat next to my mother as she cried all the way from California to Idaho. We moved from an upscale neighborhood with a private tennis and swim club into a single-wide trailer. But we were safe, and life began to come into my mother's face a little at a time, day after quiet, nondramatic day. The ordeal had turned her from blond to completely grey in one year's time. She reentered the job market after nearly 15 years at home.

We all held out hope that Dad would check himself into rehab and get help. We all desperately wanted to repair this fractured family, but he continued in the denial. Eventually he met another woman and began the whole insane, dysfunctional cycle all over again.

But Mom didn't. She was determined to get emotionally, spiritually, and physically well. She was determined to help all of us kids get the help we needed to overcome the chaos of our home so we could have healthy marriages and families some day.

Enough Is Enough

There are a few key decisions my mother made that has turned her into my hero today.

Confront the issue. Although it took her a long time to gain the strength to do it, there came a day when she had to say to herself first, *Enough is enough. There is a better way to live, and we need to take that path.* She didn't want a divorce, and she didn't want another man. She just wanted to find a new way to live for herself and her children—a safer, saner way to live.

Confront the involved parties. With love and concern, she laid out clear choices. She explained which healthy path she was taking and offered that path to all of us who were involved. Then the choice became ours (and Dad's).

Confront the past. There was nothing she could do about all the years of chaos to move us all forward. She had to give herself mercy, but she didn't ignore the past. She went for counseling so she could learn from past choices and behaviors and not repeat unhealthy patterns.

Confront the future. I watched as she continued to do whatever was best for her children. I heard her make choices such as:

1. *This is not about me. It is about my kids.* I watched Mom make

all of her choices with one thing in mind: kids first. She separated with hope that Dad would get help, so she didn't run right into a divorce. Once the marriage ended, she refused to date until (1) she was emotionally and spiritually well and completely healed, and (2) my siblings graduated from high school. She had friends, but no boyfriends. She didn't want to further complicate my siblings' lives.

2. *God is bigger than my problems.* I saw her read more than a hundred Christian books that first year. She got us all back into church, and she developed a routine of daily Bible study. She did whatever it took to gain a bigger view of God and rebuild her strength and confidence so we kids could lean on her if we needed to. In the process, we all learned how to lean on God.

3. *I will focus on what I have, not what I lost.* She kept choosing joy and hope. She gave to friends, family, and her community, and this helped her rebuild her stamina and future. Instead of giving in to fear, she decided to view this as a growing adventure with God. She experienced a series of firsts. First time to be the one to check the family in at a hotel; first time to drive anyplace out of town alone; first time to rent a car, then buy a car, then buy a home.

4. *I will grow as a person.* Mom knew that in order to move us forward in life, in order to rebuild her marriage if Dad got his act together, in order to provide for us on a daily basis, she had to grow and grow quickly. She sought counseling, a support system, and invested in many seminars, conferences, books, and Bible studies to learn new tools for a new way of life.

Confronting a Person

No matter if it is confronting an issue or a person, the act of confronting is an emotionally difficult and often draining experience. In our book *Every Marriage Is a Fixer-Upper,* we encourage people to avoid (1) *accusations* (name-calling and guessing at a person's motives); (2) *generalizations* (you *always* do that; you *never* do this); and (3) *rationalizations* (you would have done the same thing as me if you knew how much stress I was under...then some excuse is given).

Heart-to-Heart

When I need to confront a person, I first ask myself this set of questions:

1. Whose issue is this (who absolutely needs to be at the meeting)?

2. What is the best time to discuss it? (Pick a time that is unrushed and when people involved are rested and, if possible, happy or at least not emotionally volatile).

3. Where is the safest place to have the discussion? If the person is easily enraged, a more public setting (counselor's office, restaurant, living room with at least one loved one present) will be safer. If the person is calm, the conversation can and should be held in a more private location.

Then I like to use a simple diagram to write out ahead of time my thoughts, emotions, and words before the hard conversation takes place.

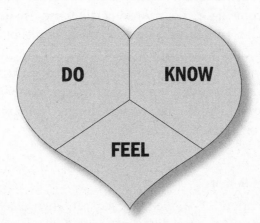

Know. What do I know to be true? What are the facts? Treat this section as though you were a police detective or scientist sticking only to what you can observe. For example: *I see you are coming in later and later. I have observed you are getting thinner, have more*

headaches, grades are going down, etc. I have noted that you have been slamming the door, throwing things, etc.

Feel. First, go through your own feelings before you ever say anything to anyone. Are you angry, hurt, frustrated, or disappointed? Take those feelings to Jesus. Ask Him to fill up those emotional needs in your heart. Don't expect the person whom you are confronting to ease the pain of any of your emotions. If they were good at that, chances are you would have never had to have this hard conversation.

Second, put yourself in the person's shoes you are going to confront. How do you think they are feeling (fearful, frustrated, defeated, out of control)? When you confront them, what feelings do you anticipate receiving back from them (anger, shame, denial)? You can't judge anyone's motives or guess at someone's feelings, so you will need to ask questions in the conversation to try to draw this information out of the person you are confronting.

Do. What do you desire this person to do? More importantly, what do you think God wants done? What is it you will or won't do if they (1) respond well, (2) if they don't? You may not have all the desired outcome figured out ahead of time, and usually it is best if you don't go in with a full agenda to push. You should, however, have some idea of what behaviors, actions, and decisions you feel God is leading you to in response to the current status quo.

When I use this little simple diagram, it gives me time to think and pray through all the decisions, feelings, and ramifications of the situation instead of just reacting.

A Word About Parents

Confrontation is a whole other subject when it comes to your aging parents. The main difference is that you want to work at acceptance really hard first before you ever bother to confront anything for two reasons: One, they are your parents. They deserve honor and respect simply for bringing you into this world. Two, they are older and might be set in their ways. The chance of them making dramatic life and behavior changes is slim to none. You will want to remember when you are getting older that flexibility, growth, and willingness to change are attractive traits that will draw your loved ones closer to you instead of pushing them away.

Here are some tidbits of advice from the members of our Seasoned Sisters group who have experienced being a caregiver for their parents.

Give honor whenever possible. Compliment your parent often on what a fine job they did raising you. This will come in handy when you have to say, "Mom, Dad, you did a great job raising me to be a wise, discerning woman. I am asking you now to trust the job you did as parents and listen to some recommendations I have for your future well-being..."

Touch often. Pat, stroke, hug, and kiss. When you get irritated, decide to do it. Your emotions will follow your good decisions, so decide to continue to be affectionate.

Pull resources. You don't have to be the only one involved in caring for your parents. Rally a meeting of your siblings, your parents' sisters or brothers, and even nieces and nephews or grandchildren who care about your mom or dad. If everyone does a little to help carry the load, then no one will be overburdened. If someone's work doesn't allow them to give time, they may be able to give money to help defray costs. One sister, who had no time to invest, paid the other sister, who had time but little money, to be a full-time caregiver. In this way, when the primary care giver needed a break, she had some funds to hire qualified help.

Help them stay independent. Give your parents responsibilities as long as possible. Even making their own toast will give them a reason to wake up, climb out of bed, and get dressed. Assign them a flower bed to tend, or ask them to read (or simply tell) the grandchildren bedtime stories.

Get help. Many communities have senior centers, hospice, and other resources for the elderly. Know what is available in your area.

Have a prayer team or friendship circle to encourage you as you care give. On Monday morning each week, four of us Seasoned

Sisters send a weekly prayer update. One of the women on the update is a caregiver, so we pray for her parents and her labor of love each week. Just having a few friends who care and encourage can help you maintain perspective. If any of your friendship circle has done caregiving, their wisdom will benefit you, so ask if you can take a friend to lunch, or meet her for a prayer walk, and listen to her wisdom.

Caring Confrontation

If you do need to confront a parent in order to help them maintain a safe living environment or in order to help them stay alive, ask the person in the family with whom the parent has the strongest relationship to run the conversation. It is also nice if that person has the longest fuse because anger and impatience are usually counterproductive. You all might decide to be there to answer questions or lend support, but have the person who has the best relationship try to negotiate the tender topic first. If it all goes well, the whole family can bless that mediator with some special thank-you. If it doesn't go well, then you can gather a few more family members together and try again.

In the end, as long as your parents aren't a harm to themselves or others and are still mentally competent, they are in charge of their own lives. Even if you are not thrilled with their choices, these are their lives. What you do have control over is how you will give your time, your money, and your emotional energy. Pray about what God wants you to do and when. Make your choices according to what you sense God is asking you to do, rather than through family shame, guilt, or even personal worry.

Accept that People Grow and Change

One of the sad facts in our lives is that our kids will leave home. Often, when we women reach our forties, we begin to realize we have drifted into people pleasing and long to maintain control in our children's lives. We are used to being needed, and we long to be just as important in our adult children's lives as we were when they were growing up. As we feel appreciated less, it is easy to become resentful and entertain thoughts such as:

- No one understands me.

- No one cares what I do.

- I knock myself out, and for what?

- I always have to do everything.

- It's all on me.

- The world would come to a screeching halt if I didn't show up.

- I'll show them—I just won't do it!

It is also easy to fall into the habit of adding side comments to all our acts of service, such as:

- Told you so.

- See, you should listen to your mother.

- What would you do without me?

- Who loves ya, baby?

- If you'd only listen.

Before we know it, we have adopted a martyr syndrome. We are sold a bill of goods by the devil that the world will come to a screeching halt without us, our input, our direction, our opinion, our...shall I say it?...control. We complain about the work we have to get done, all the while wearing it as a badge of honor and prestige. I know. I've been there. I can so easily fall into the martyr syndrome. The big problem with being a martyr, however, is all good martyrs usually end up dead.

I recently heard Sarah Groves in concert, after which I sent a copy of her CD *Station Wagon* to each of my kids with directions to play the song "Small Piece of You." It's a touching story of a young mother looking at her baby and picturing how hard it would be to let go as her baby grows. And with Sarah's unique ability to bring the whimsical and humor into her work, sprinkled throughout are these one-liners:

> Go on, son, and see the world. I hope you see it all;
>   But please, please, please, *don't forget to call...*

> Go on, son, and spread your wings. I hope that you take flight;
>   But please, please, please *don't forget to write...*

> I know that it's not fair to hold you down, now is it?
>   So please, please, please *don't forget to visit.*[2]

I laughed out loud when the chorus in the background rang out in harmony, "Do you have any idea how painful childbirth can be?"

The reality is that our kids will grow up just the way we did. They will become responsible adults who perform much better in their homes than they ever did in ours. Even if they started poorly or made unhealthy choices along the way, they have the potential to change at any time. Early in life, our kids are who they are because of our choices on their behalf. As they get older, they become who they are because of the choices they make. Our job is to make the adjustment from being their guidance counselors to being their cheerleaders.

Let Them Launch

In our home we have a series of traditions that show our teens and young adults that we are releasing them to run and be responsible for their own life. The first tradition is actually a simple question. When they are tweens (around 12 to 13 years old), if they want a new privilege, or the privilege to go someplace new, we say to them, "Tell me why I should say yes." Then we ask them to come up with a list of questions a healthy parent would ask and bring us the answers to the questions. We roll the ball back into their court, forcing them to take responsibility to think through their life. Usually they either realize it is not a good idea, so they let it drop, or they do a thorough job in presenting their case. If it isn't illegal or immoral, we'll usually say yes. In the teen years, we want to save the nos for the really big, life-altering issues.

Bill and I explain our parenting philosophy in *The 10 Best Decisions Every Parent Can Make*. Each year we negotiate privileges and responsibilities with our kids. Part of this process is to have our teens preset their own consequences if they don't follow through with their agreed-upon responsibilities and moral choices. In doing this, we take ourselves out of the bad guy role because the teens are forced to take responsibility for their decisions and the consequences of poor choices. Our goal is to have them own their life by the time they are 18. Remember, we are trying to work ourselves out of a job.

At 12 or 13, our sons complete a relationship contract which has them answer a series of questions to prepare them for guy/girl relationships. (The contract is also in *The 10 Best Decisions Every Parent Can Make*.) Then at 16, when they get their driver's license, we give them two gifts. The first is an ID bracelet with 1 Thessalonians 4:3 on one side *(This is God's will, that you abstain from sexual immorality)* and the phrase "Until the Day," on the other side. They are also given a key chain with these same things on the two sides of the key chain. It is our way of reminding them that we are trusting them to use this new privilege to drive to places of purity and to places that will help them and their friends grow with God. Our prayer is that they choose to remain sexually pure until their wedding day.

We also make a big deal out of their eighteenth birthday. We pray over them as we give them a special photo album with memories from their life and a Bible that has been marked by us with passages we think are vital for their future. For example, in the Bible are notes in the margin like, "This is my (Mom's) favorite verse. Ask me why" or "This passage helped me through a really hard time. Ask me how." Or in the book of Ruth, I write a question over each chapter heading. It has four questions. Ruth 1: "Ruth made an excellent decision, what was it?" Ruth 2: "Ruth is an excellent woman, what are her traits?" Ruth 3: "Boaz is an excellent man. Why?" Ruth 4: "There is an excellent outcome. What is the happy ending and why did it happen?"

When they leave for college, we have a series of five meals with them and discuss what we call "The Freshman Foundation" (also in *The 10 Best Decisions Every Parent Can Make*). And we have a few "Farrel Family Traditions." For example, our Farrel Family Scholarship Fund has these requirements for endowment:

1. We consider college education a partnership. You should do all you can to save money or earn college scholarships and we will do the same. In the spring of your senior year in high school, we will sit down and together decide what options are available to you based on money and scholarships. At that time, we will tell you what amount of money we will have available to you to help fund your college education. College is a privilege, not a right. After 18, we as parents legally owe you nothing, but we believe in you and will invest in your future.

2. Mom and Dad work too hard to fund sin. If you decide to walk away from the faith (our guidelines are: no drinking, sleeping with a girl, drugs, or illegal activity), then you will be on your own to fund your life. All financial help (cell phone, use of the car, money for school, books, or housing) will be gone.

3. Mom and Dad do not fund mediocrity, negative attitudes, and excuses for anything less than your personal best. If you select a Christian college, you will fully participate in all character-building activities (chapel, class attendance, homework, church, Christian service, etc.). If you select a secular college, you will create a similar setup to ensure spiritual growth so that you are best prepared for life following college. This spiritual growth plan will include:

a. Being mentored, either one-on-one or in a small group, by a spiritual leader with our family's theology

b. Weekly corporate worship (any service that works in your schedule)

c. Some kind of Christian service using your gifts

d. A regular personal devotional life (the goal is a daily time with God, but a devotional time a few times a week is minimum. We will ask you what God is teaching you and that is how we will gauge if you are connecting to God.)

If we see you are rebelling, and you are confronted and you do not repent, we will follow the Matthew 18 mandate, and in the end, if you still don't respond, you will be on your own to fund your life. But at any time you want to get right with God and the family, there will be a room for you at home to regroup and come up with a plan for your future. If you are simply choosing mediocrity, you will be given a "probation period" to reprioritize your life. If we see improvement, and you have a plan in place for future improvement, we will work with you to keep your education in place. If, however, there is no improvement, we will consider it rebellion, and we will proceed with the steps under number 2 above.

When you deal with "worst case" scenarios ahead of time, when everyone's excited about going away to college, and all the fun planning is going on, it will be less painful then, and in the future, if you ever have to use the "contract." We've only had to use the "mediocrity clause" so far, and I think in part it is because our sons knew we were dead serious about the rebellion-equals-no-money clause.

We have also seen contracts like this work if grown children live with you. One mom had a "cleaning clause" in her contract. Instead of getting angry that her grown daughter was a slob, the mom simply hired a maid and charged her daughter half the bill.

Some parents charge rent; others offer to lower rent if the grown child helps with chores at the same level of excellence a person hired would do them. You decide what will help your son or daughter be best prepared for a strong responsible adult life.

You Are on Your Own

For the most part, Bill and I keep the transitions and traditions on the positive side and celebrate the releasing of responsibility. For example, between the ages of 18 and 21, when we feel our grown child is ready, we have a "walk into manhood." For Brock, it came when he went away to college as a freshman. We invited his role models, coaches, and mentors to come to a day where they each brought a quote for a scrapbook. Each walked the football field with him (Brock was a college quarterback), complimented his character, and also explained the meaning of being a man. Zach's was later, at 21, when he got a new truck when away at college. He had a "drive into manhood" where he drove with his dad and older brother to visit each mentor so they could give Zach their wisdom. Caleb, who is currently 16, will also have a personalized entrance into manhood when the time is right.

Every parent has a point when they must release a young person completely. This point is usually marked by a decisive change in the financial arrangement we have with this young adult. When our kids are in college, we give them the exact date that we will no longer be helping them in any way financially. We tell them, "On this date, you will own all responsibility for transportation, cell phone, insurance (car and health), all your bills, housing, etc." We work to gradually give more and more of these financial responsibilities over to them year after year throughout college.

Because we highly value marrying while sexually pure if at all possible, we tell our children that we will give them the same amount of money whether they are married or single in college. We were college pastors, and we have worked in relationship ministry, so we do a lot of premarital counseling. We have seen too many young adults feel that their parents wanted them to finish college first before marrying, which is a nice logical goal for parents to have. However, these young people loved Jesus, loved each other, and loved their parents. To ask a young couple in our sexually saturated world to date two, three, four, or more years and expect them not to fall into temptation is a tall order. Some couples might manage to do it, but I believe parents should consider the big picture. A healthy marriage relationship, a sexual history without regrets, and a college degree will all have equal value as time passes.

When our son Brock married, at the reception we gave him and his bride a prayer walk where people could walk and pray over the young couple. Then later we gave them a card with a check in it to help them establish their new life—and two "apron strings." We had a "cut the apron strings" ceremony complete with Bill and me praying over them as a couple as they launched into their new life.

In *The Afternoon of Life,* Elyse Fitzpatrick shares a letter that she encourages a young couple to write to each set of parents:

> Dear Mom and Dad,
> I want to thank you for your love and devotion to me as I was growing up...At this time, a very important time in each of our lives, our relationship will change—not deteriorate but change, not disappear but be altered... As a Christian I will always honor you, appreciate you, respect you, pray for you, commend you and seek to help you, but still God says I must leave...From the time of our wedding onward...I ask you to help us to learn how to merge our two independent lives into a one-flesh relationship practically...You have been given wisdom from God, and from time to time we will be turning to you for counsel. When we do, we will take your counsel seriously, but under God we will think, search the Scriptures and pray, and determine God's will for ourselves...We want you to be free to agree or disagree with us...and we want the same freedom.... [3]

The In-law Dance

Recently I have been interviewing women who have multiple daughters- and sons-in-law to see what works best for them. One wise woman told me, "I have four sons and four daughters-in-law, and every relationship is different. One of my daughters-in-law wants me to know everything. She wants me to be included in all of the family's events and special occasions. Another is very private and even resents questions that I think simply show interest, care, or concern. The third moved my son halfway around the world for her career, but she is loving, giving, and calls often. I think she feels bad that they are so far away. The last born married a girl with 'daddy issues,' so she is young and insecure and easily offended. I usually don't know I did or said something wrong until I run into some unseen line I crossed."

I love my daughter-in-law. I know she is God's perfect woman for my son. I love her parents, her siblings, her values. But that doesn't mean there haven't been adjustments. Any marriage is the merging of two families, two sets of traditions, two sets of inside jokes, two family's schedules, and two family's personalities. One family may be loud and enthusiastic, while the other is quiet and conservative. One family may be open and candid about personal issues, while the other prefers to keep things private. One family may be easygoing with childrearing, while the other is controlled, disciplined, and regimented. One may be liberal and generous with money, while the other may have experienced financial trauma or simply be tighter with their funds. There are many new decisions the young couple will need to make, so you will be more appreciated by your new in-law if you give the newlyweds plenty of time and space to forge their new life together.

The Hiccups

For the most part, these traditions, coupled with a few other key, proactive, parenting principles we talk about in detail in *The 10 Best Decisions Every Parent Can Make,* lay a strong foundation for launching responsible adults, but there can be hiccups along the way. We always pray that they are "recoverable" mistakes that do not dramatically alter the course of their life. Let me give you a more comical example of a "hiccup" in one of our son's journey to responsibility. All of our kids have had and probably will have "hiccups" on their path to maturity. Even when you are a proactive parent, they still have to own their own life and take over responsibility, sometimes one painful step at a time.

Our son, Zach, is the captain of his college athletic team because, even as a junior, the coach saw he was the most responsible one. We teach the principle that the best thing about you can become the worst thing about you if you don't monitor the gift. Zach is great with people. He is also gifted at counseling, so he is always the one everyone calls if they have issues. All that was well and good until early in Zach's college life, when Bill got Zach's cell phone bill. We give the kids "x" amount for cell coverage as a gift to their education until they finish college. We are a spread-out family and have to travel so much for our ministry that we want to be able to get hold of them easily. Well, Bill got a bill for $150 over the allotment, and it was all from text messages! He called Zach and told him, "I don't know whether to be upset with you or proud of you. I am not even sure how you could have been involved with that many text messages and keep up with college and cheerleading." Then the next month, we got a bill for $250 over! Bill was livid, but instead of calling when he was angry and feeling emotionally out of control, I offered to talk to Zach.

"Zach, let me try to explain how we are feeling about this—"

"I am so sorry, Mom. I'll pay you back." He interrupted with a hug.

"I know you are sorry, but I still want to explain how we are feeling." Then I went on to explain feeling disrespected, not listened to, etc. Then I said, "Zach, what we really want to know is your plan to not let this happen again."

"Mom, I am so sorry. (Hug) No problem, I will work overtime, and I will get this to you as fast as I can." The entire conversation happened as I was stepping out of the car to catch an airplane home after a visit to Zach. Before I even got to the security gate, Zach had called my cell again.

"Mom, I just want you to know I called the phone company and got my text message turned off so my friends can't text me anymore. And I called Dad and told him I'd work overtime and I estimated how long it would take me to get the money to repay you. And, Mom, I apologized to Dad and I just want to tell you thanks for loving and supporting me through college. I will never take advantage of you again. I love you." We all know that these kinds of promises are not guaranteed, but I was glad to see the attitude of his heart. He paid us back sooner than he promised. Internal attitude had turned into external action. And that's really what you are going for, everyone's heart being in the right place.

That's why I practice proclamation prayers. I proclaim the truths I *want* to be true about me, about my life, and about my children's, family's, and friends' lives. For example, if a child is struggling with foolish choices, I pray verses about wisdom out loud. If I am finding it hard to love a person because they are acting unlovable, I proclaim verses of love over both of us. By using proclamation prayers, I see life as it should be lived and how God intended for it to be lived, not just as it is being imperfectly lived in the here and now. As I pray the truth about life and people and myself, new ideas, creative ways to resolve conflict, and compassionate caring methods to deal with difficult confrontations appear. It is as though proclaiming the truth is a powerful rushing river that carves out a new, better way to act and react to people, and the place the river leads is to the calm heart of God.

Joy Choice

Use one of the methods talked about in this chapter to prepare for a difficult-to-have conversation you have been dreading. And when you have a difficult conversation planned, ask a trusted friend to pray for you while the conversation is happening. If the person is open to it, pray before and during your conversation with them. Prayer, just by its very nature, tends to calm the waters.

Calming the Chaos

*It finally dawns on you that really and truly
your parents are not perfect. Never were
and never will be. And your children are
not perfect. Never were and never will be.
And you are not perfect. Never were but
maybe someday...no, never will be.*

Wouldn't it be nice if, whenever we messed up our life, we could simply press Ctrl, Alt, Delete and start all over? In the last chapter we talked about caring enough to confront and accepting that people grow and change. In this chapter, we will extend the CALM in our lives by learning how to forgive and move forward.

Learn to Forgive, Reconcile, and Release

In order to protect your own character as you have to deal with hard conversations and people who are difficult to love, you will want to become a master at forgiveness. This is an area Bill and I have taught on for many years because we have seen God's amazing grace and forgiveness firsthand, up close and personal, because of the homes we grew up in. We know our "Redeemer lives" (Job 19:25). God takes the difficult and makes it easier, captures bad and turns it into good, transforms the unhealthy into healthy, and turns negative into positive. I am not sure how He does it, but God takes the broken things in life and somehow makes them better and useful for His purposes. The transformation process for the situations of your life begins with the act of forgiveness.

We looked at the greatest act of forgiveness, what Jesus did on the cross, and asked, "How can we translate this into help for interpersonal relationships?" From that question, my pastor husband created Six Steps to Forgiveness.[1] If you can truly walk through these six statements for a specific act or word, then you have "forgiven." The only thing left to do is to forgive that person for the next hurtful thing they may do.

There is a lot of confusion over forgiveness. We all know we should do it, but we're not sure what "it" looks like. Sometimes we think forgiveness is just letting the offense go, but we've seen that people don't know where to let it go or how to let it go. Other times, people think forgiveness is sweeping the offense under the rug with the phrase, "Let's just not talk about it" and pretend it never happened. That isn't forgiveness; that's denial. Sometimes we don't forgive because we think forgiveness means we must reconcile. But forgiveness and reconciliation are actually two separate acts. Forgiveness is a vertical act, a private prayer that takes place between you and God in response to a person's actions. Reconciliation is a horizontal act that involves forgiveness on the part of the person who was offended and true repentance by the person who did the harm. It is extremely difficult, and unwise, to reconcile unless you have first experienced the vertical act of forgiveness with God.

Six Steps to Forgiveness

1. *I forgive (person) for (offense).* This statement is a reflection of 1 John 1:9 (NIV): "If we confess our sins, he is faithful and just and will forgive us our sins and purify us from all unrighteousness." The idea is that we are to specifically confess the sins that stand in our way of an intimate relationship with Jesus. In the same way, the more specific you can name the offense of another, the more specific the healing God can send to your heart. For example, you wouldn't say, "I forgive my husband for being a jerk!" Instead, list

off the "jerky" behaviors so you know what it is you are forgiving and then God will send His hope and healing into each area of pain and hurt. (Plus, this step is helpful if reconciliation does occur because you will know what issues need to be addressed.)

2. *I admit that what was done was wrong.* This statement is a reflection of Romans 3:23 (NIV): "For all have sinned and fall short of the glory of God." We don't like to say anything is "right" or "wrong" these days because we live in a politically correct environment, but if nothing is done wrong, then there's nothing to forgive and perhaps it is just your bad attitude that needs adjusting. Besides, this statement puts you in the "gritty" state of mind that is necessary for forgiveness. Forgiveness never feels good, so we need to be determined that those who did wrong will never win.

3. *I do not expect (person) to make up for what he has done.* This statement is based on 2 Corinthians 5:17 (NIV): "Therefore, if anyone is in Christ, he is a new creation; the old has gone, the new has come!" Jesus does not require that we make up for all that we have done wrong before He forgives us. Instead, He provides a "do over" point where everything can begin anew. Lots of time women live their lives "on hold" waiting for the person who wounded them to come back and throw themselves at their feet and beg forgiveness. Give it up, girl! Chances of the people who wounded us coming back to say they are sorry are pretty rare. And even if they do come back, is there anything they can do to take back their words or actions? Nope. To be able to move yourself ahead, or to move the relationship toward reconciliation and repair, you have to let them off your hook.

You may be thinking, *That is so unfair! Why should I let them off the hook?* Well, if they are still on your hook, they still have emotional influence in your life. Do you want the person who wounded you to have that kind of control over your emotional well-being? Besides, the Bible says, "'Vengeance is Mine, I will repay,' says the Lord" (Romans 12:19). God is all-knowing, all-powerful and Almighty. He can think of all kinds of creative ways to make someone miserable and repent much better than you. Just give that person who has wounded you over to God to deal with. (However, keep in mind, if there is going to be reconciliation, they will need to return and own their issues and apologize—that is reconciliation. And reconciliation works best when there is forgiveness first.)

4. *I will not use this offense to define who (person) is.* This statement is based on Romans 8:9: "However, you are not in the flesh but in the Spirit, if indeed the Spirit of God dwells in you. But if anyone does not have the Spirit of Christ, he does not belong to Him." God defines people as either "in Christ" or "separated from Christ," rather than classifying people by their sinful behavior. This one is tough. It is so easy to point to the person that caused the pain and say, "That's the person that ruined my life (stole my happiness, ripped off my opportunity for success, broke up my family, etc.)." But if she is the person who "ruined" your life, that makes her like some big monster ruling over your world. It's as though she is the puppet master and you become the puppet. She is a victimizer, so that makes you the victim. Who wants to go through life with a victim mentality? I'm hoping you don't because it sets you up to be revictimized over and over again.

So remove the labels and simply see that person as God does, "in need of a Savior," or in need of walking with the Savior she claims to know. This will shrink that person down to size. She will no longer be a monster, just a pathetic person in desperate need of change by the hand of God. There is only one person who is in worse shape than you are with your pain, and that is the person you are seeking to forgive. She may be in a clueless state, not realizing how she offends or hurts people, or worse, she may realize it and not care.

I, for one, do not want to empower these kinds of people in my life. How about you? God has many ways of working out consequences in people's lives and really does not need my help. Be content to know that if someone mistreated, betrayed, or wounded you, they are training those in their world how to mistreat, malign, and wound. Eventually they will be the recipient of their own devices.

5. *I will not manipulate (person) with the offense.* This statement

is also based on 2 Corinthians 5:17. In making all things new, God has chosen not to manipulate us into doing His will. Instead, He calls us by His love to walk in new life. This is you choosing to give up pressing buttons or pulling out the trump card and saying, "I remember 70 years ago when you did this to me!" If you still have to manipulate someone, they have emotional control over your life. Take the high road instead of manipulation or revenge. Remember, we don't forgive because people deserve it. We all deserve hell. We don't forgive because it is good for the other person. No, we forgive because it is good for us! Forgiveness frees us to go forward in life and in all relationships in a healthy way. Forgiveness creates an ambience that attracts healthy, emotionally well, and stable people into your world. Forgiveness works like a magnet to draw in the happy and positive people.

6. *I will not allow the offense to stop my growth.* This statement is based on 2 Peter 3:18: "Grow in the grace and knowledge of our Lord and Savior Jesus Christ." God does not expect us to be perfect, but He does expect us to grow. The most important step in forgiveness is the decision that the junk stops with you. Decide to do whatever it takes to move forward in life: counseling; meeting with a pastor, director of women's ministry, or prayer partner; or getting in a small group that deals with specific pain.

A great quiet time activity is to pray, "God, show me who and what I need to forgive" and then list any hurt and pain that comes to mind. Don't overwork the list because forgiveness is a lifestyle, not a one-day event. Jesus will bring situations to mind as you are ready to forgive them. As you consistently ask Him and then walk whatever He brings to mind through these six statements, you will develop a heart that is free of bitterness.

Real Reconciliation

You may be saying, "Okay, now that I have forgiven, then what?" The Bible is pretty clear that we are supposed to try to make things right between us, if at all possible.

Matthew 5:23-24 (NIV) says, "Therefore, if you are offering your gift at the altar and there remember that your brother has something against you, leave your gift there in front of the altar. First go and be reconciled to your brother; then come and offer your gift."

Matthew 18:15-17 (NIV) shows the flip side. If you think someone has hurt or offended you, Jesus gives an order of events or meetings that works best in a caring confrontation. "If your brother sins against you, go and show him his fault, just between the two of you. If he listens to you, you have won your brother over. But if he will not listen, take one or two others along, so that 'every matter may be established by the testimony of two or three witnesses.' If he refuses to listen to them, tell it to the church; and if he refuses to listen even to the church, treat him as you would a pagan or a tax collector."

God is saying that reconciliation works best when it is a two-way street. If you realize you may have hurt someone, apologize, own the issue, and ask, "What will make things right between us?" If someone has hurt you, the Bible gives you a few options, based on how emotionally safe that person is and how volatile the situation is at the time. Matthew 18 says to go to the person individually and have a private interaction. If they don't respond well, take another person with you and go again (it is usually best if the second person has some authority or clout in the person's life: youth leader, pastor, best friend, mentor, counselor, older respected relative, etc.). If they still don't respond, "Tell it to the church." If it gets to this stage, you will want to share the information with the key person who is in a position of spiritual authority in this person's life (if there is one). You are not responsible to change this person's attitude or behavior—you are responsible to be Christlike toward them (so pray and ask Jesus what that will look like).

Good Wins

Once you have forgiven, you will be in a position to "overcome evil with good" (Romans 12:21). Remember the story of my dad? I decided that if he said and did hurtful things, I would still act toward him the way a loving daughter would act, regardless of his actions toward me. In this way, I would protect my own character and not become callous or hard. I did, however, set boundaries for my safety and the safety of my kids. If he drank, I didn't stay all night with him. I wasn't a passenger in his car. I didn't allow my kids to be exposed to his unhealthy patterns, so if he began to act unruly, it was time to go.

With each interaction and boundary set I'd ask, "What best protects my dad and his relationship with me and our family?" For example, I didn't ride in the car with him if he drank because, if an accident happened and someone got hurt, I knew Dad would be so overcome with grief, guilt, and shame he would be suicidal. Sometimes the person doesn't feel blessed by your choices and boundaries, but the needs of those closest to you are more important and the offender may come around over time.

One way to bless them is to look for neutral territory. If it is a child or a spouse, breaking all ties would mean their hope for repentance would be unaffected by your influence, and you might be the only example of light in his or her life. Finding activities you can agree on can help or rebuild the relationship. Let me give an example. Linda was a new believer and each of her teen children came to faith in Christ, the oldest just a few months before her own engagement. The daughter decided to move in with her fiancé, who was also a believer but, obviously, not walking with God. Linda was in a quandary. "Do I go to the wedding showers? Do I do the usual wedding festivities, even though their choice to live together is not pleasing to God?" After much prayer and talking over the issues with her spiritual mentors, Linda decided that (1) living together was not God's will, (2) the marriage was a good choice, (3) the couple was young in their faith, so it would take time to move into maturity, and (4) after the couple married, special memories would build into the relationship with Mom and with God. After considering all those variables, Linda decided to take the following course of action: She would explain God's plan of engagement to her daughter (live separate and no sex until the wedding night) and anything to do with the wedding she would support and participate in, because having a wedding, getting premarital counseling, and preparing well for marriage were ideals she could endorse and support.

The common ground became attending church, planning the wedding, and attending the wedding showers and celebrations. However, she explained to her daughter that she would not socialize at the apartment. The two getting married were paying for their own wedding, so in this case there wasn't much of a financial consideration, but for you, pulling back financial contributions for certain activities you feel uncomfortable with is certainly an option because it is money God entrusted to you for good use.

The book *Boundaries* by Dr. Henry Cloud and Dr. John Townsend is very helpful for times like this. For example, if you are married to an unkind, verbally abusive spouse, then when he swears, simply state, "I do not deserve that kind of language. I am going to leave this conversation if you swear at me again (or call me a name), and I will walk out of the room." Then if he does it again, walk away. This can also work with teen or adult children.

Or, if your mother continually belittles you or undermines your authority with your children, explain your feelings once and then see if she changes behavior. If she doesn't change, then explain what consequences will happen if she continues. In our family, we have a family member in our extended family who is mentally unstable and won't get help, so we had to institute a 60-minute visit rule. We noticed that if we stayed in her company 60 minutes or less, she didn't have time to become outraged or out of control toward us or our children. If the visit was in public, say at a restaurant, it seemed she could hold it together for about 90 minutes. Instead of overnight visits, we did stopovers of shorter length. As a result, we were all able to maintain a relationship with this person. Having the boundary salvaged the relationship.

Protect Your Heart and Ability to Do Ministry

Sometimes certain people are so hurtful and emotionally unsafe that you might need to take the boundary to the next level. Jesus said, "Do not throw your pearls before swine" (Matthew 7:6). That doesn't mean the people are pigs. It just means if you keep going back over and over again, sharing your heart over and over and over and they just keep hurting you, justifying, accusing, or saying more hurtful things, then don't go back to them anymore because, for the time being at least, it is useless. It is as though your heart is full of precious pearls and they are stomping on it. God doesn't want you to be subjected to that kind of treatment because it reinforces bad behavior on the other party's side. You do not have to set yourself up to be revictimized.

One woman I met while speaking had to quit sharing personal information with a friend because every time she was vulnerable she found that the information was not kept confidential. More often than not, it was used against her in a future conversation. In a friendship, this usually means you just decide to not spend time with that friend. In a family, it may mean you only spend time in a large family setting where you can choose to keep the conversation on the lighter side, or where you can simply be polite but spend time with other family members who are more trustworthy.

In the worst of circumstances, God then encourages you to release that person to Him completely. Romans 1:24 (NIV): "God gave them over in the sinful desires of their hearts." The context of this is the particular sin of homosexuality, but it matches the words of Jesus in Matthew 18:17 pretty well when He said to treat the person as a "tax collector or sinner," meaning you treat them just as you would treat any person on the street you don't know. You don't hang out with them because they will hurt you again, but you are giving them common courtesies, such as saying hello or holding open a door. You quit commenting on their choices or behaviors and basically let natural consequences take over. The time of trying to rescue them or redeem the relationship is over. At this point all you can do is pray and treat them the way you would any stranger you met on the street.

I have found that for most people, most of the time, the very first step is all that is needed—go to them and bring up the issue. Most people don't mean to hurt you. However, in very difficult cases, the Matthew 18 process and the following steps may mean a series of meetings. If you work all the way through the process and the person still hasn't owned their side of the issue, or is completely unrepentant or hostile toward you, then this person has become "unsafe." For the time being, it isn't wise to have much interaction with him or her. Just pray and give God time and space to work with him.

Move Yourself Forward

If you want to maintain peace in your heart, you must commit to personal growth. No matter who you are, or what devastating age you are going to be on your next birthday, your life is getting bigger. The people around you have confidence in you, so life will require more of you each and every year. If you grow to keep up with the demands, you will enjoy the next season of life and live with a deep sense of satisfaction. If you refuse to grow, life will overwhelm you and encourage you to panic and give in to the stress. Women who move forward seek to reach their potential. They believe they are God's workmanship, created in Christ Jesus for good works that they should walk in them (Ephesians 2:10).

Tennis, Anyone?

Women who move forward own their *own* responsibilities and refuse to take on the responsibilities of others. Candy squeezed in her weekly tennis game, forcing herself to slip away from her home-based business office. She knew she needed the exercise but wasn't sure she should keep up the appointments because her plate seemed so full. As she stepped off the court, she stopped at the Tennis Club restaurant for breakfast with friends. But nothing seemed all that appetizing. *Lord, that's how I feel about life right now. Everything just seems, well—blah. Like I'm living life in black-and-white in a color TV world. Father, I just feel so "heavy."*

An inaudible voice seemed to whisper, *"Then roll the ball back."*

Roll the ball back? She pondered those words. Joe and Karen came up and said, "Hey, Candy. Where's your husband? I know he's busy, but he promised he'd get me those numbers I needed—for your lawyer and that company you used for home security."

"He's been swamped. I'll get those numbers to you today myself."

Candy dashed from the club to the middle school to pick up Terri, her daughter. She wasn't greeted with a "Hi ya, Mom!" Instead, Terri barked out commands of, "I need this and I need that and I need it right now!"

By the time they got home from errands, Cliff, her high school son, drove up in the driveway. "Hey, Mom, did you get my uniform washed?"

When Candy walked in the house, her arms laden with groceries, she noticed that her college daughter, Kelly, was watching TV while the kitchen sink was full of dishes. There was no sign of any dinner being prepared so, as soon as Candy lugged in the groceries, she began to chop vegetables for a salad. Terri bounded down the stairs with, "Mom, we forgot poster board and my project is due tomorrow." Her husband came home, gave her a quick peck, and asked, "Did you pick up my dry cleaning today?" Then Cliff, carrying an armload of dirty sports gear, came in, tossed the clothes right onto the kitchen counter, and said with an attitude, "Mom, they aren't washed! I need them in the morning." Then Kelly walked in and said, "I'm hungry. What's for dinner?"

Roll the ball back! The voice inside her now transformed from a whisper to a scream. She pictured herself out on the tennis court and, with a powerful forearm, she whacked the ball back into her partner's side of the court, making her chase the ball.

Put the ball in their court, Lord? Is that what You are saying? She got the picture. She realized she had been taking on everyone else's responsibility, owning everyone else's issues, covering for everyone's mistakes. So, in her mind, she lobbed those responsibility balls right back over the net. She sensed an affirmative smile from the Holy Spirit inside her heart.

"Cliff, you know how to use the washer. I suggest you start the load."

"Kelly, you can finish dinner since you are so hungry."

"Terri, Dad would love to drive you to get the poster board. The store you need is right next to the cleaners."

"I'm going to jump in the shower, and we'll all meet back here for a family dinner. There's something I'd love us to talk about tonight!"

She gave her husband a kiss and whispered in his ear, "Thanks for running Terri to the store. While you are there, if you want to pick up some massage oil, I think we might be able to find a use for that later tonight." They both smiled as she went up the stairs.

She felt light again, and it seemed as though a rainbow of color was being brushed back into her world from heaven.

One Wise Choice After Another

One of the major choices we have during life's second half is to clear up any chaos sent our way by making a series of wise choices. Jesus said, "Love the Lord your God with all your heart and with all your soul and with all your mind...Love your neighbor as yourself" (Matthew 22:39 NIV). There are three people to love listed: (1) the Lord, (2) your neighbor, and (3) the hardest one to do, yourself! Sisters, we need to value ourselves the same way God does or life will pile up on us like snow on a rooftop—and eventually a neglected emotional life will cave in on you.

Jenny tried to pull herself out of bed one more day. She had a new job, but going seemed overwhelming to her. Every morning for the past few weeks she'd tried to talk herself into life, saying, "Come on, you can do it. Get up and get going." But going seemed to be something that just wasn't going to happen this particular morning. She was weary, discouraged, depressed, and felt in a fog most of the time. She was trying to do her best as a mother, a friend, the head of household, and as an employee, but this day she hit the wall and could go no further. Jenny says, "I had reached the end of myself even as I clung to God. I picked up the phone and called a friend I *knew* would see and hear my cry for help!"

Life had stacked up on Jenny. In the past five years she had dealt with her mother, whom she was very close to, being diagnosed with cancer, so Jenny flew between states to care for her and took care of the sale of her property two months later after her mother's death. Two of her children graduated from high school, so she had gone through the grueling college scholarship application process with them. During this time, she discovered that her husband of 21 years had multiple addictions and he refused treatment, instead choosing to plunge himself and the family into chaos and danger. In the end, the marriage ended in divorce. This meant Jenny needed to help provide for two kids in college, so she took a couple of college computer courses and reentered the workforce. Then her favorite sister-in-law, who supported her through the divorce, and her favorite aunt, who helped her care for her mother, both died of cancer.

Then, six weeks prior to hitting that wall, within a four-day period Jenny found out that someone had fraudulently set up bill paying on her bank account and withdrawn $3400. Then a sheriff called stating she could be liable for a motor home her addict ex-husband had bought, and she had a very upsetting conversation with her son's girlfriend, and the next day her son called to tell her he didn't want her to contact him. Not see him, no phone calls, nothing. Jenny reflects, "That was the topper. I was devastated. My sons are my treasure here on earth." Seventeen days later she was laid off from work. She had become victim of one emotional hit-and-run after another. She had secured another job, but now she found herself unable to even get out of bed.

Jenny shares, "I had nothing else to give. I was an empty shell. I needed someone to take care of me, but my mom was gone, one son had walked away, the other was unavailable due to college responsibilities, so I called a best friend. She came right over. She held me. Rocked me. Listened to me. Allowed me to sit silent and just receive her prayers over me. She took me to the doctor the next day, made my appointments for a counselor and psychiatrist, went with me to my first counseling appointment, and then called a few other friends to become a support team for me."

One friend drove Jenny to her first psychiatrist appointment and completed disability paperwork and other tasks that just seemed overwhelming, while others prayed for her, came by to visit, brought her flowers and food, took her to lunch, and expressed the love of God in human form.

As Jenny looks back, she sees that the warning signs of a meltdown were there, but she didn't recognize them: confusion, weariness, lack of energy or excitement. She tried spending more time with God, reading, and going to Bible study, but her ability to concentrate had evaporated. She said, "I would start to pray and end up just asking God to hold me because I had no energy. I was not blaming God and knew He was always right there.

"My best friend had said that first day when I called her, 'You have had a dump truck land at your house. Everyone has come first, but it has to be your turn now. Taking care of you is priority number one. You love people, but you aren't responsible for them. Now God wants you to take care of you. Let Him come minister healing to you. He did it for the prophet Elijah who gave it all and then was hit with emotional depression. God even sent birds to bring him what he needed. God will do that for you. To start, let's have you hit your wellness in a multifaceted way. You are body, soul, and spirit, so let's put together a plan to rebuild you in all those areas.'"

That's what Jenny did. She pulled together the best resources. She met with her physician, got a psychologist and psychiatrist, and it was determined that she was suffering from a form of posttraumatic stress, which led to depression. She learned that this is much more common among midlife women than is talked about. People sometimes joke about the much-prescribed Prozac, but few talk about why so many woman are taking it. She also met with her pastor and signed up for a Life Skills class. She took a sabbatical from work and added physical exercise, rest, and personal spiritual replenishment with books, Bible study, and praise music to her life. She was on medicine for a short time period while her body regained its natural strength. She spent time with friends who were positive and affirming. She hung on to the truth that "with God all things are possible" (Matthew 19:26), which included rebuilding herself and her life.

Jenny writes, "Close to 15 months have passed since I made that first phone call to my best friend. In the beginning I wondered if I'd ever be the same. I know now I will never be—and that is a very good thing. God continues to change me, heal me, and grow me, and I like the me I'm becoming. I've learned I need someone to take care of me—me. It's important to take care of myself so that I can be available for God to use me. It is not being selfish.

"And God reminded me of so many things. My weariness came from carrying everyone's responsibility on my shoulders. No one asked me to, I just took it upon myself. What a freedom comes from unloading that which does not belong to you. I was not doing anyone else a favor. Actually, I was hindering their growth and hurting myself in the process."

As Jenny began to take better care of herself and learn new ways of relating to those in her world, all her relationships were strengthened. "Two months after I received that devastating phone call from my son, we talked, reconciled, and redefined our relationship, which I find is ongoing with adult children. Ten months ago I started a new job, which has stretched me and grown me. It is a miracle too, as it is a job God gave me having had no experience in that area at the time. The same awesome God also allowed me to refinance my house during the time I had no job—a miracle! He continues to be faithful, providing for all my needs at the perfect time."

God laid the rungs of the ladder for Jenny to climb out of the pit life had pushed her into. Every good decision leads you to the opportunity to make another good decision. Freeze right where you are, sweet sister. Take inventory of your surroundings. Is God asking you to make a decision that will set you on a path of wholeness, adventure, and emotional, spiritual, and physical wellness? It's one step at a time.

Can You Hear Me Now?

Women who move forward seek God for direction. They believe

that Jesus was serious when He said, "Seek first his kingdom and his righteousness, and all these things will be given to you as well" (Matthew 6:33 NIV). One of my friends, Kathy, hit a hard spot in life after her fortieth. She'd already lost her dad, then her marriage hit a rough spot, then her mother passed away. To jump-start her forward movement, God asked her to take a radical step of obedience. She writes about her road less traveled.

"One morning I fell apart, crying out to God, 'Why am I so frantic all the time? Why do I always feel I have a to-do list a mile long and I can never get anything finished?' I was actually serious this time in expecting an answer. I had angrily yelled that out before but didn't stop long enough to wait for an answer.

"That morning, as I began to wait for an answer, that in itself a rare thing, the still, small voice inside me whispered, 'Spend an hour with me daily for 30 days, just listening.' Sarcastically I mused, 'Oh, that should be easy. I can't even get the things done I need to get done. Where was I going to find an hour of time to do that?' But it was a distinctive voice I could not ignore. So I surrendered my time to the Lord and asked Him to show me how that would look daily.

"Morning by morning, as I had journal and pen in hand, the Lord dramatically spoke words of encouragement, discipline, direction, and wisdom to me. I was directed to Scripture for my children and thoughts to pray for my husband. I was reminded of the weaknesses I needed to change. My home was strengthened by this time in a powerful way."

In that year of listening, God reminded Kathy of the amazing things He could do when her ear is finely tuned to His voice. She reflected on one day in particular:

"I was curling my hair in the bathroom and a powerful thought came over me. 'Ask your sister if she wants to know Me!' It was so distinct that it caught me by surprise. I proceeded to tell God how that would be so uncomfortable and how she already thinks I'm a Jesus freak, and on and on with the list of excuses of why I could not do that.

"But the thought would not let up.

"Meanwhile, my sister was on her way over to my mother's house. I was staying there for a season as my dad was in the hospital losing his battle to prostate cancer. I needed to update my sister that morning of the latest details from the doctors. It seemed there was nothing more they could do for Dad.

"My sister and I had no relationship because of home dynamics growing up, so this time of suffering was actually the first real emotional connection we had experienced. But she still thought I was a Jesus freak, so the mention of anything spiritual seemed so beyond what *I* could do.

"Once she arrived, it was a very quick visit. She was dropping off her kids to run to her work responsibilities. I briefly shared with her the difficult news that we had to face with Dad. We both shed a brief tear, and then she glanced at her clock and said hurriedly, 'I have to go!'

"Knowing this was my last opportunity to do what I believe God was putting on my heart, I eloquently yelled out from the porch as she was halfway to her car, 'So, if you want to know any more about Jesus, just let me know.' I wondered if she felt as though it came out of left field because there had been no mention of Jesus in our conversation that morning.

"She did a 180-degree turn and said, 'I do.' Shocked, I sat down with her on the grass that warm spring day in May and told her an encapsulated version of who our loving Savior is. I then asked her if she wanted to accept Him into her heart. Without hesitating she said yes. And this 'Jesus freak' had the privilege of ushering her into an eternal relationship with our Lord and Savior, all because I stepped out to listen and obey that still, small whisper I heard in the bathroom that morning."

God has told each of us, "Call to Me and I will answer you, and I will tell you great and mighty things, which you do not know" (Jeremiah 33:3). What is Jesus whispering to you?

— *Joy Choice* —

Which of the ideas to bring CALM hit closest to your heart? Select one idea and begin praying about how to implement it into your life this week.

Humorist Leigh Anne Jasheway writes in her book *I'm Not Getting Older (I'm Getting Better at Denial)* that you know you are in midlife if:

- You think you still look twentysomething. From the back. At night. In the fog.

- The words "for someone your age" don't need to scare you. For example: "You certainly have nice legs for someone your age" isn't too bad.

- You can look at the glass half empty. You can look at the glass half full. Or you can look at the glass and wonder, "Did I or didn't I just drink my soy milk?"

- This is the year you've decided to be adventurous. Why not get a tattoo? A tattoo of your address and phone number could not only be attractive, but very useful in those memory emergencies.

- [You are] looking for a new exercise program. Try the Memory Loss Workout. Go to the kitchen. Now, try to remember why you're there. Walk back to the living room. Try to find your keys. Okay, breathe.[2]

Monitor Your Money

If your outgo exceeds your income, then
your upkeep will become your downfall.

I asked my friend Ellie Kay, America's Financial Expert, to share a wealth of her wisdom (pun intended) for all of us seasoned sisters over 40 who might need a bit of advice about our pocketbooks. Ellie Kay is the bestselling author of nine books. My favorites are *A Woman's Guide to Family Finances; Shop, Save and Share;* and *The Debt Diet.* She has appeared on CNBC, CNN and *Fox and Friends,* and is an international radio commentator for *Money Matters.* She is a columnist for *Today's Christian Woman, Lily Magazine,* and *Military Spouse Magazine.* Ellie Kay is married to Bob, currently a corporate test pilot and a former Stealth F-117A fighter pilot. She has five children and two stepchildren, so this former military wife knows how to save money and make it stretch![1]

In our book *Men Are Like Waffles—Women Are Like Spaghetti,* Bill and I make the case that the key need in a woman's heart is the need for security in all the important areas of her life. She longs for security in her relationships, in her home surroundings, and as she ages, financial security becomes more and more important. No woman wants to fear being put out on the streets or becoming a burden on her children as she ages, so wise financial planning and honing her financial skills is a vital growth step. Here is Ellie's advice, with a few of my thoughts, and a few other resources, interspersed.

Ellie shares how her financial expertise began:

When I was in the eighth grade, I was 5 foot 8 inches tall and weighed 125 pounds. I was a petite size 8. Life was a lot easier when my problems were smaller than my waistline. I was simply too young to appreciate how good I had it. It only took five pregnancies and 20 years for me to fully appreciate my eighth grade year!

During that time, my friend Donna (who was also petite) and I convinced ourselves that we really needed to lose five pounds. Thankfully, my Spanish mom had a no-nonsense approach to life that helped me get a grip before I could even think of falling into the teen trap of perfect bodies and eating disorders.

It all started when Donna and I made ourselves accountable to each other to only eat nutritional foods and forgo sweets. But my *mamacita* had a plan. She whipped up my favorite chocolate cake, knowing full well that I couldn't resist the sweet indulgence. Later that day, my mom drove Donna and me to the mall and, much to my horror, my mom proceeded to tell Donna, in her heavy Spanish accent, about my misdeed:

"Today, Doo-na, Ellie, she no so good."

Donna was polite. "What did Ellie do that wasn't good, Mrs. Rawleigh?"

"Today, Ellie, she each de cho-co-laa-te cake. She shee-it on her diet!"

I was mortified over my mother's pronunciation of "cheat." It came out of her mouth as a combination of "sheet" and a well-known four letter word of similar sound.

Later that day, I pulled my mom aside. "Mom, can I talk to you a moment?"

My mom stopped dusting the coffee table and gave me her full attention. "Chure, what do chew want to talk about?"

I didn't quite know how to broach the topic, so I just blurted it out. "Well, Mom, it's about your accent."

"What ax-cent? When I *first* come to de United States of Amer-eeka, I haff an ax-cent. But I no have no ax-cent no more!"

Despite her denial, I was a teenager on a mission and trudged on. "I know, Mom, you've really lost a lot of your accent. But there are still some words that you don't pronounce correctly. And when I'm around my friends, the way you say certain words embarrasses me!"

Mom was genuinely concerned, "Well, I no embarrass you for no-thing! You tell me de words and I will practice dem!" The rest of the day, as she cleaned house she practiced her enunciation skills. Each time she dusted the lampshade, cleaned the bathroom mirror, and wiped down a kitchen counter, I overheard her saying, "My daughter, she *shee-it* on her diet."

Going on a Debt Diet

Whether you're talking about diets or debt, cheating in any language can get you into trouble. And when it comes to finances, many Americans have been toting around sizeable debt and need to go on a "debt diet"—and stick to it! Just like the woman who uses a girdle to "shift the weight around" in an attempt to look thinner, poor money managers have their own "weight shifting" devices that appear to make the debt load seem lighter than it really is.

I call these debt shifting techniques "Dumb Money Moves" because they remind me of some silly rabbits in a children's book called *The Dumb Bunnies*. These cwazy wabbits do things like pour porridge down their pants, wear underwear on their heads, and open the door in an attempt to get a tan. Going off a diet can be embarrassing in more ways than one.

Sadly, many women seem to be reading from *The Dumb Bunnies Guide to Financial Management*. What are some ways that people shift the burden of their debt to try to make it appear less than it really is?

Fiscal Fitness Workout

Consider the following ten statements. In either attitude or action, rate the range of your agreement by answering "agree," "maybe," or "disagree."

Top Ten Dumb "Money Moves" Quiz

1. I have a large mortgage because all mortgage debt is good debt.

2. I'll just use a home equity loan to pay off credit card debt.

3. I'll put it on my credit card.

4. I need to drive a really nice/new car because it will save on maintenance.

5. We always get a big tax refund.

6. I'm going to borrow from my 401(k)/IRA. I'll look into the details later.

7. I'm not building my 401(k) in this kind of market.

8. I like/invest in this company because I know them.

9. I don't want to contribute to a nondeductible IRA because there's no tax benefit.

10. I should probably refinance, but it really seems like a hassle.

Answers: Top Ten "Dumb Money Moves" Quiz

1. *I have a large mortgage because all mortgage debt is good debt.* **Disagree.** One major reason for debt gain has to do with the "good news/bad news" of recent mortgage rates. According to Economy.com, annual household liability has grown 24 percent since the start of 2004—which is 10 percentage points *more* than during the 1991 recession. Part of the increase can be attributed to the enlarged number of homeowners today—which we all know is "good" debt. It's kind of like the dietary equivalent to having muscle weight instead of fat weight—and we all know that muscle weighs more than fat. However, when it comes to finances, at some point the good debt/bad debt logic is going to break down.

For example, the mortgages that many homeowners have today are much larger than they might have been in the past due to lower interest rates. Furthermore, many homeowners have taken advantage of rising home values to use some of their equity to pay off consumer debt such as cars and credit cards.

On the one hand, "People have improved their balance sheet because the mix (of debt) is better," said Brian Nottage, Economy.com's director of macroeconomics. "If people are going to rack up debt, better that it's mortgage debt."

The interest rates on home equity lines of credit (HELOCs) tend to be much lower than credit card interest rates and the interest rates are usually tax deductible. Since the risk of not paying your mortgage means a possible foreclosure, the incentive to pay those debts are greater. But what happens when the rates follow the norm of adjusting upward? If you also have a mortgage rate that is adjustable, it means you could suddenly see your debt load rise significantly, and that means more debt weight than ever before.

If home prices slow down or the companies downsize and individuals lose their jobs, debt-laden consumers could find themselves clamoring to work off their debt load in order to fit into the "size eight jeans" of that lovely new home or car.

2. *I'll just use a home equity loan to pay off credit-card debt. Disagree.* I alluded to this in the previous paragraph, but why, specifically, is this a Dumb Money Move? Lenders love to tout the benefits of using Peter to pay Paul. And when home equity rates are down, it seems like a good move, right? Wrong. According to the Federal Reserve, last year we borrowed $701.5 billion from our home equities, which is up $416.2 billion from 1997. The only way this truly helps is if you completely stop using credit cards to run up those debts—an act of discipline which the average American will simply not commit to. Therefore, unless you're well above average, it's not a good move. Your debt hole is getting deeper, and you don't even realize it because you're able to keep making your mortgage payment and don't see the bottom line of your total debt load.

You want proof? According to moneycentral.com writer, Liz

Pulliam Weston (January 28, 2004), "Nearly two-thirds of the people who borrowed against their home equity between 1996 and 1998 to pay off credit cards had run up more card debt within two years, according to a study by Atlanta research firm Britain Associates."

This slowly whittles away the equity you have in your home for use in case of an emergency, such as unemployment, medical expenses, or other financial setbacks.

3. *I'll put it on my credit card. Disagree.* If your credit card works out more than you do, you likely have a debt weight problem. For example, some consumers feel that by using their credit cards for daily purchases they're building airline miles or they have an interest-free loan until the bill comes due. But buying on credit makes it far easier to overspend, by buying just a little more and thinking about it later. Paying cash is a more conscientious decision, no matter how you look at it. Plus, fees are becoming more and more prevalent. The average woman is less likely to buy whenever the urge hits if she's constantly forking over $20 bills to pay for purchases.

There are two kinds of debt: good debt and bad debt. A mortgage is an example of good debt; consumer debt is the bad kind of debt. Your credit card debt may either be in the card or in the mortgage—but the debt is still there, waiting to be erased.

According to CardWeb.com, at the end of 2004, the average family's debt load was $8940. That's expensive weight to carry around, making the family more at risk for an average of 16.2 APR for most cards. The amazing fact is that the average family has not only one card, but 16! That typically includes six bank cards, eight retail cards, and two or three debit cards.

4. *I need to drive a really nice/new car because it will save on maintenance. Disagree.* We are in love with cars. The American fantasy includes a big house, nice cars, and dream vacations. While we might get good interest rates on our home and economize on vacations, it's usually the car craze that loads us down with debt in the end. Auto sales have been at near historical levels in the past

five years, and the average consumer has paid more than ever for the privilege of owning a cool car.

According to the Consumer Bankers Association, the size of a new vehicle loan has increased 5 percent to $21,779 in 2002. The average size of a used vehicle loan rose 12 percent to $16,542. The trend toward longer loans means that the average consumer will have a car that will not be paid for in less than 49 months. By the time you trade in the car for a new one, the old car is often worth less than the loan value and the trade-in value adds debt upon debt, if you feel you have to have a new car every five years, which most Americans do.

Is it only car and mortgage weight that is weighing us down? Unfortunately, no. We have smart people making Dumb Money Moves that keeps them from paying off debt, even when they have the means to do so.

5. *We always get a big tax refund. Disagree.* The operative word here is "big," meaning more than $2000 or so. If you are getting this much back in a refund, then you are likely overwithholding on your taxes. Some people just like getting that check every year so they can spend it on vacations, luxury items, or paying off an item they bought in anticipation of the refund. Most tax professionals are exasperated with clients who are getting upwards to $10,000 in refunds and are happy about it. It's usually best to adjust the W-4 to have less withheld rather than having the "forced savings" of a refund. That way, your money makes money throughout the year, instead of sitting stagnant, waiting for you to get it back in the form of a refund.

6. *I'm going to borrow from my 401(k)/IRA. I'll look into the details later. Disagree.* The younger the family, the more likely they are to make a Dumb Money Move without knowing the details (penalties, restrictions, and limitations involved) of their financial decision. Let's say a family takes $50,000 in early distributions (withdrawals, not loans) from a 401(k) or IRA to buy a home because they thought they could do so without penalty. Without knowing the details, they don't realize they are wrong in their

assumption. You can only take a $10,000 distribution from your IRA without penalty if you're a *first-time home buyer* and even then you'll *still owe income tax.*

It's amazing how many long-term decisions are made as a result of getting casual (and bad) information over a watercooler conversation. One young family man believed he would pay a 10 percent penalty for everything he withdrew over $10,000 from his 401(k) in order to buy a home. Instead, he ended up owing taxes and penalties on the whole amount. It's important to check with a tax professional before you make major financial decisions. The end result in the case of this young man is that the family got tagged with a $19,000 tax bill because they didn't check the rules and run the numbers before making the withdrawal.

7. *I'm not building my 401(k) in this kind of market. Disagree.* Don't deprive yourself of a tax-deferred savings plan for the future because the market is down today. Furthermore, you shouldn't deprive yourself of free money if your employer is matching the contributions. Even if the market is down, you don't have to invest your 401(k) in stocks. You could put your money in a low-risk bond or money market fund until the market bounces back.

8. *I like/invest in this company because I know them. Disagree.* Suppose a doctor is fond of investing in a particular pharmaceutical company because she is familiar with their products and services. Is that a good reason to buy their stock? No. Similarly, employees tend to own too much company stock because they're overconfident they'll know when to sell. They feel they'll see the writing on the wall internally. I'll sum up that faulty logic in one word: Enron.

The best advice is still to never invest more than 10 percent of your portfolio in any one stock and never more than 30 percent in a particular sector, even if the company is owned by your mother.

9. *I don't want to contribute to a nondeductible IRA because there's no tax benefit. Disagree.* The individual ends up not investing in *any kind* of IRA at all and the future will not fund itself. The money you put into an IRA might not be tax deductible, but the interest that grows from that fund is still tax deferred. This means

the money can grow faster than it might in one of the taxable accounts, where you'll pay taxes every year on dividends, capital gains, and interest to Uncle Sam and to your home state.

10. *I should probably refinance, but it really seems like a hassle. Disagree.* The only reason you should not refinance isn't because of the hassle, but because of the bottom line. If you crunch the numbers on the amount of time it takes to shop for a loan, fill out the paperwork, and project the overall benefit, then you'll find it truly could be worth the hassle. For example, if you can save $3600 per year with a refi, and the process takes about ten hours, then you are making around $360 an hour! This is guaranteed income (and tax free, I might add) and usually worth the time. Just make sure the numbers add up to your advantage in order to make this a smart money move for you.

Assessing Your Debt Diet Needs

Give yourself one point for every question you answered "agree," two points for "maybe," and three points for "disagree."

Financially Fit:

If you scored between 26 and 30, then you weren't swayed by any of the gimmicks or tricks found in the money moves that were suggested and you are financially fit (not to mention *smart*).

Mild Problem:

If you scored between 22 and 26, then you have a mild debt problem and may want to lose a few pounds to be at top form.

Moderate Problem:

If your score was between 18 and 22, then you are susceptible to making some Dumb Money Moves that could keep you in debt for most of your life. You most likely live above your means and have a mounting debt problem. A smart move would be wise to develop a better understanding of debt and begin a path toward the right attitudes and actions that will help you improve your financial status.

Major Problem:

. If you scored less than 18, then you clearly have a significant debt problem that will weigh you down and keep you from reaching the finish line of your financial goals. You need to take deliberate, disciplined action to overcome the problem. If you continue down the path you are currently on, you will likely end up in need of the financial equivalent of gastric bypass: that is bankruptcy and/or no retirement funds or a financial future to pass on to your children. But even in your case, there is still hope for your future.

This test is not scientific and it can be subjective. Whether you need to lose a few pounds of debt or a truckload, the good news is that you are reading this chapter. So take heart! This could very well be the time when you understand where you are, how you got there, and how you can regain your financial health. (Thanks for the *Debt Diet* tips, Ellie!)

Rounding the Bend

From my vantage point (this is Pam speaking now), as we women head into the second half of life, lowering our debt is one of the smartest steps we can take to feel more financially secure. But getting to that low debt ratio may not be very easy. You may have college expenses for all your children, weddings to host or attend, graduations to celebrate, and grandbabies to buy for or get on a plane to go see.

It is easier to be motivated to save, cut costs, and be wise stewards when we have a goal in mind. Let's take an obvious goal we should be mindful of: retirement. By retirement, I do not mean stopping work. I actually believe work keeps us alive longer. For my book, *The 10 Best Decisions a Woman Can Make,* I ran across numerous studies that showed that those who volunteered outlived their less-involved peers. I want to stay active and involved, and that's also a core value of Seasoned Sisters, because it is better for us and the world when we do.

Recently, while listening to the news I heard this story:

> Arthur Winston usually drives to work, but today he decided to take the bus. Mr. Winston turned 100 Wednesday, but that's not the only reason for all the hoopla. As CBS News correspondent Bill Whitaker reports, it's also his last day on the job. He is retiring after 72 continuous years at a Los Angeles bus yard. Even more remarkable, Winston is retiring with his unblemished work record intact. It was this incredible record that first drew CBS News to Mr. Winston when he was only 98.
>
> Back then, we noted that this cleaning supervisor at an L.A. city bus yard had never been late, never called in sick, never punched out early. It was the best work record the U.S. Labor Department had ever heard of.[2]

"Winston missed one day of work in over 70 years, and that was to attend his wife's funeral in 1988. In 1996, he received an 'Employee of the Century' citation from President Clinton."[3]

One month after retirement, Arthur died.[4] (Yeah, I know—he was 100! But it does show that sometimes, if we have a reason to get up in the morning, we do.)

So many of us may work, even later in life (two-thirds of workers say they expect to continue working at least part-time in retirement.)[5] In the Bible, people served and worked right up to death. For the believer, our secular career might end, but God still expects us to employ our talents in serving Him and serving humanity. We should all, therefore, look at retirement as a career *change* because God knows that having purpose and meaning in life keeps us alive and engaged so we can better enjoy life's second half. Work itself can be good, but wouldn't it be nice if we worked because we *wanted* to—not because we *had* to?

How Much Is Enough?

To plan for the later part of life's second half, start with a retirement dream. You can't plan if you don't know what you are aiming for. What kind of lifestyle and what activities do you want in your golden years? Traveling the world? Puttering in the garden? Starting your own business? Staying involved through part-time work? Launching your own business or ministry? Early retirement to sit on the beach and recover from years of overtaxing and overscheduled work? Pursuing a long-awaited hobby? Downsizing your home or relocating? Spending time with grandchildren? Volunteering? Staying in shape? Dancing the night away in some exotic location or simply reading about it and hosting a book club? What is it you want to do in your retirement? After you have an idea or picture of how you will spend your days, then you will have a better idea of what you will need to fund it. Other factors to consider:

- The age at which you plan to retire.

- Your life expectancy. (A doctor might be able to help you gauge this one, but in the end, the Bible makes it clear that God is in charge of how many days you will have on earth. Current statistics reveal that in the U.S., average life expectancy at birth is about 79 years for women and about 72 years for men.[6] So if you retire at 65, then you need to plan on at least 14 more years, and life expectancy is increasing each year, so planning for 20 more years is prudent. If you retire earlier, add more years to the equation.)

- Social Security benefits expected, as well as the amount and type of employer benefits (if any). To check your estimated Social Security benefits, contact the Social Security office and ask for a Personal Earnings and Benefits Statement. It shows your earnings records, work credit, and estimate of benefits. For information on your pension plan, talk to your company's human resource management office.

- The amount and growth rate of your savings and investments. (Adjust retirement costs and growth rates of
  investments with inflation. Inflation in the past 20 years
  has averaged approximately five percent a year.) Project
  the average rate of return of investments and how much
  personal savings you will have accumulated by retirement age. Include the value of other potential resources,
  such as income from part-time work, inheritance, business interests, or real estate. It may be helpful to discuss
  the details with a financial planner to calculate the value
  of these assets and determine investment growth and
  projected income needs.

Once these variables are identified, the amount of additional
money needed can be calculated mathematically. If you are not a
math whiz, invite a friend over who is and do a few calculations. To
determine savings requirements, subtract your annual Social Security estimate and any other inflation-adjusted retirement income
sources from your annual retirement income needs. This will give
you the amount you must fund with investments and employer-
sponsored or personal savings plans. After considering the amount
you'll receive from other investments and pension benefits, compare
your financial resources to your retirement income needs. Understand that the resulting calculation at this point is a rough estimate
that does not account for inflation.

There are many churches that provide seminars on estate planning, and often there is a retirement component to these, and many
times these seminars are free. In addition, there are many financial
planners who specialize in retirement planning. (And as in taking
care of your medical health, getting a few opinions is a wise choice.)

After you have a number in mind, you can then make plans to
save the required amount of money. To reach your retirement goal,
it is critical that a dollar figure be attached. If you have a designated
date for retirement, and a preset amount needed by that date, then
the next step is developing a plan to break down that financial goal
into bite-sized pieces (amount needed to save or invest per year or

per month), and you have created a basic financial plan. If current and projected resources won't provide sufficient income, you'll need to make adjustments. Options might be: increase savings, include increasing income with a second career or part-time work, reducing expenses, increasing the return on your investments, downsizing to a less expensive home, retiring later, or lowering your projected standard of living in retirement.

Some of you might need motivation to sit down and create this retirement plan. One of my dearest friends was procrastinating, but she finally made an appointment with a financial planner. At the meeting she discovered she could retire five years *earlier* than she thought! She has now sold her home in a pricey real estate area and downsized to a beautiful new but smaller home right near her grandchildren. In her grandchildren's lives, those five years meant Grandma would be there for ballgames, gymnastics meets, and the significant markers of getting a driver's license, going to a prom, and middle school and high school graduations. You might be surprised by your plan if you just sit down and do it.

Funding the Dream

Scott Reeves of *Forbes* magazine recommends you start by saving 10 percent of your net income—make it 10 percent of your gross income, if possible. He says, "Take the 10% off the top and budget household expenses as if the money didn't exist—in fact, have your employer deduct it before taxes so you won't even see it and be tempted. You'll get an immediate 30% bonus for not having to pay taxes on it now. Some employers will even match some of this in a 401(k) account."[7] More than two-thirds of workers favor automatic enrollment in 401(k) plans, which is a great idea because you can't spend money you cannot see.[8] (Even if you are self-employed, you can create an automated savings plan.)

It will be hard emotionally to pay yourself first. Even if money is tight and you are saving for other goals, regularly set aside money for retirement. Keep in mind, children may obtain scholarships and student loans to finance their education, but scholarships for retirement don't exist. Besides, it does young people good to struggle to earn their way in school and in early marriage years—most likely you did. Give them the same opportunity for personal growth and development. Otherwise, their personal growth might be providing for you in your old age—and honestly, there are no guarantees they will want to or be able to—even if you were Mother of the Year!

Obviously, the earlier you begin to save, the better. For example: If you're 30, earn $30,000 a year and save 6 percent of your salary each month, or $150, and if you earn a 10 percent average annual return, you'll have $569,495 at age 65. However, if you start saving at age 55, you'll accumulate only $30,726 in the next ten years.

Learn about your savings options. For example, some IRAs are tax deductible and some are not. You don't receive a deduction for contribution to a Roth IRA, but this is offset by the value of tax-free withdrawals. A Roth IRA allows you to withdraw assets without the usual 10 percent early withdrawal penalty—if you use the money to purchase a first home, for college expenses, or if you become disabled.

After educating yourself on options (stocks, bonds, investments, real estate, IRA, Keogh, etc.), draft a plan by calculating how much you and your spouse are likely to need in retirement and identify potential sources of income. Conservative financial planners typically say that you'll need 60 percent to 80 percent of what you earn during your career in retirement, but more experts these days are recommending 80 to 100 percent of your annual salary should be what you accumulate to live on in retirement. It all depends on the lifestyle you prefer while in retirement and if you have an income stream from any kind of ongoing work or investments during those later years. Keep in mind, the early years of retirement, called the active phase, are the most expensive. (Because you are out having fun!) But health care costs, if you suffer from a drawn-out battle with cancer or Alzheimer's, can be unbelievably high as well, so both issues should be kept in mind.

Decisions, Decisions

There are many decisions that you will be making in life's second half and in planning for it. For example, if you sell a home in California and retire in small-town America, your profits from a home sale can help you purchase a comparable or downscaled home and still have a nest egg left over for retirement. However, if you plan to stay in the family home and it is not paid off, then you will continue to have mortgage payments each month, and that will affect your income needs in retirement. You can downscale needs and desires because some costs can go down: clothing, commuting, and the cost of raising kids, but keep in mind that you're likely to want to spend more on travel and gifts to grandchildren. You should also plan to spend more on health care, even if you have good insurance coverage.

Your primary sources of income in retirement are likely to be Social Security, company pensions, private savings, and investments. A note on Social Security: 49 percent of workers—and 44 percent of those 55 and over—mistakenly believe they'll be eligible for full Social Security benefits from one to four or more years before they actually are, and with the ever-changing political scene, the age of retirement under Social Security may go up again. On average, workers still rank Social Security as one of their largest expected sources of retirement income, but with the boomers coming into retirement, don't bank too much on Social Security.

And corporate retirement plans are not as stable and reliable as in past years, either. Forty percent said they or their spouses have a defined benefit plan at work (such as a traditional pension), 61 percent somehow expect income from such a plan in retirement. And 37 percent expect to receive retiree health insurance, another unrealistic assumption when many employers are curtailing or eliminating this benefit.[9] Remember, often the retirement plan at work is only as reliable as the company. With Enron and Tyco scandals in the back of our minds, it is wise to take some of your retirement savings into your own hands. But if you do have a reliable employer benefit plan available, maximize it. Employee contribution plans, such as 401(k) and 403(b), can build significant retirement funds. Contribute as much as possible. Saving just one percent more of your pay adds up with compound interest, so take full advantage of employer matches, if offered. This is free money that should not be passed up.

If you're self-employed, you definitely need to be assertive: contribute to a Keogh, IRA, stocks, bonds, mutual funds, or certificates of deposit. It's also time to draft a will. Consider creating a family trust to save everyone the headache of probate. Talk to an estate planning attorney to see what documents will best secure your family's future. (If you have children under 18, a will also declares who will care for your children.) Set aside an emergency fund to cover three to six months of expenses. An emergency fund can prevent the need to dip into your retirement contributions for extra money and face the resulting penalties and tax obligations.

Are you ready? Most of us are not:

Wake up! More than two-thirds of workers—and more than half of those 55 or over—have less than $50,000 saved for retirement. While 70 percent of workers say they or their spouses have saved for retirement, only 64 percent are currently saving. Only 42 percent of workers say they or their spouses have taken the time to do a retirement needs calculation, and 8 percent of those say they guessed. (For help with the calculation, there are numerous sites on the Internet you can find by simply putting "retirement planning" in a search engine.)

Only 39 percent of workers think they need to accumulate at least $500,000 for retirement, and 30 percent say they can make do with less than $250,000, an amount that invested at 5 percent would generate only $12,500 a year. Many women may think they need very little for a comfortable retirement because they have not really thought through the retirement planning issues. Don't guess, plan. And if I may make the risk of being a Negative Nelly, plan on a worst-case scenario. Financial expert Matthew Greenwald aptly reminds, "Many who expect to work may not be able to. Past surveys have consistently found that about 40 percent of workers quit before they want to because of 'negative' reasons, such as health problems or layoffs."[10]

Wise up! Create a savvy mind-set. Diversify. With the help of a financial planner, consider educating yourself on stocks, bonds, savings plans, IRA, real estate, etc. Most planners look at the safety of investments to provide long-term financial stability. Keeping some money in stocks, for example, helps your retirement keep pace with inflation.

"Continue investing after retirement...Make tax-efficient asset withdrawals in retirement. After retirement, keep money in tax-deferred accounts as long as possible. Make withdrawals from taxable accounts and bonds before tapping into tax-deferred investments. Withdraw wisely. Many financial advisers believe retirees can logically plan for a withdrawal rate somewhere between 4 percent and 5 percent annually."[11] Retirees should base withdrawal decisions on expected investment returns and the desire to leave money to heirs. (For example, what is your philosophy on leaving an inheritance? Are you going to own an RV with a bumper sticker that reads, "Spending my children's inheritance" or are you more likely to scrimp and sacrifice so that your children and grandchildren have college savings or help with a down payment on a home?) Determine how much help you want to be able to give and when you will give it ahead of time, and communicate this to your family.

What a good financial plan will do is take out as many hardships and surprises (especially negative ones) as possible. The Bible makes it clear that financial planning is a good idea (Luke 14:28-30) and it is equally important to trust God as your provider and protector (Philippians 4:19). So the balance seems to be: *Plan for the worst, and trust God for the best.* Many retirement charts and tools are free on the Internet. One easy one to use is www.free-financial -advice.net/retire-early.html.

Seasoned Sisters Save to Share

Why be financially solvent? So we can live more comfortably in our old age? Sure, that is nice, but isn't life more than lattes in the morning and a house too large to clean on our own? I like Ellie's challenge to save so you can share. God can work "all things for good." Ellie writes:

I'd like to close this chapter by sharing a different perspective on your debt. Sometimes our problems can be our salvation—or the salvation of others. When Bob and I got married, I got a "three for one" deal, a wonderful husband and two beautiful stepdaughters. But because of the financial difficulty in his previous marriage, I also inherited $40,000 in consumer debt. I couldn't see how that kind of problem could ever be construed as good.

But life has a way of turning the tables on us. We persevered, trying to do the right thing to get out of debt and still be generous in the journey. It led to the opportunity for me to conduct seminars, write books, and eventually appear on television, sharing this wonderful discovery with others.

A few years ago, I had a chance to be part of a national television show's annual "Feed the Hungry" fund-raising campaign. The goal was to feed a million people a day in the ravaged country of Somalia. The host and producers decided to put me on the air every day that week. I remember feeling so inadequate to the task, wishing that the host would just do the fund-raising by himself.

I had a talk with God about it and pleaded, "Why me? I'm just a mom. Why not send someone more qualified, like the host or a celebrity?" Although I didn't hear an audible voice, a thought immediately came to me as real as the person sitting next to me. "You must do this because people will respond more to someone they can relate to than a celebrity."

By the end of the week, a new record had been set for their "Feed the Hungry" TV campaign, and as a result more than a million people would have food to eat in Somalia. I imagined a sea of dark faces, singing and dancing for joy that their children would have clothing, medical supplies, and food to give them a chance to live.

Who would have thought, way back when Bob and I were working like crazy to pay down our $40,000 of debt that one day our problem would be turned around to help save the lives of a million strangers in a faraway land.

I deeply believe we have the ability to be free from debt and also free from the bondage of living in the shadow of our past problems. You never know what positive outcome today's problems could have tomorrow. So I would encourage you to embrace them, work through them, and let them one day become the wisdom whereby you can serve others.

I believe that we are blessed so we can be a blessing to someone else—our blessings can have the greater destiny of impacting others for good.

Closing Note of Hope from Pam

Personally, I believe every woman can become a savvy saver, super shopper, and sweet sharer. I watched my own mother recover financially after an unwanted divorce. My mom, who worked years in banking, now ministers to other women who need to rebuild their lives. I asked her to give advice to women over 40 who find themselves in less than desirable financial circumstances:

> Always save, even if it is just a little every week or every payday. I put $10 a month in the IRA, and then I realized I wasted at least another $10, so I invested it too. And then the bank offered a 401(k) and they matched my investment up to 6 percent. I was amazed how fast that saving grew. Having some savings seems to give you power to control the emergencies and keep a single woman from panic.
>
> Go shopping and tell yourself, "I don't need that." Buy only what you need, not all that you want. Again put that money you would or could have spent that day into a savings account and feel empowered as it grows.
>
> Don't listen to every "expert" advising where to put your money. Learn where you feel SAFE with it. After 40, SAFETY is the key to saving. So many older citizens,

especially women, want to get rich and are dupped out of their savings. Go with advisors who have a proven track record of trust.

Mom also planned for rainy days so her investment in car and life insurance paid off car payments and a mortgage when her second spouse passed away. She always had certificates of deposit (CDs) in case of emergency and liquid savings ready and available so she wouldn't have to cash out CDs early and incur a penalty if hard times hit. Having savings gave her peace of mind as a single mother with three kids in college and three weddings on the horizon she knew she wanted to help with.

But it is how Mom spent her free time and social life that has most impressed me. Before retirement, she joined a ladies' investment club. Here's her spin on this "hobby," as she calls it:

> The National Association of Investors Corporation (NAIC) made it easy to start an investment club. I doubled my investment within two years but that was then, not now. The stock market is so unpredictable nowadays. The saying about stock market investing is: "Only invest what you can afford to lose." As a group of interested investors, the ladies in our group are gaining education, speculation, and adventure. To us, it's a fun way to spend $35 a month. We invest wisely and safely and then wait to see what happens. I'm the treasurer, so I track the ups and down of each stock monthly. It's fun!

Women like my mom, Ellie, and other financial advisors in your world can help you feel more comfortable and educated with your money—but only God can help you feel hopeful for a bright future, no matter what socioeconomic level you find yourself in at 40 and beyond. It is hope plus education that produce a savvy plan so you can save, feel secure, and share with others. Sweet seasoned sisters, it can be fun to be wise stewards of our time, talent, and treasure. Invest in a godly financial foundation and trust God for a fantastic future.

～ *Joy Choice* ～

Do something to be more savvy with your money:

1. Create a retirement plan.

2. Create a coupon system (see Ellie's *Shop, Save, Share* book and other money tips at www.elliekay.com).

3. Create a debt reduction plan.

4. Find out what your FICA is and plan ways to improve it.

5. Begin to tithe.

6. Create an automatic savings plan.

7. Join or create an investment club or take a class on financial management. (Crown Christian Financial Ministries offers very inexpensive and thorough options.)

11

New Horizons

When you cease to make a contribution, you begin to die.

～

Some moments in history were significant for women around the world. In 1851, Frances Gage, an abolitionist and president of the Women's Rights Convention, captured one of those moments as Sojourner Truth, a freed slave, spoke up:

> "Well, children, where there is so much racket, there must be something out of kilter, I think between the Negroes of the South and the women of the North—all talking about rights—the white men will be in a fix pretty soon. But what's all this talking about?

> "That man over there says that women need to be helped into carriages, and lifted over ditches, and to have the best place everywhere. Nobody helps me any best place. And ain't I a woman?

> "Look at me! Look at my arm...I have plowed and planted, and gathered into barns. And no man could head me. And ain't I a woman?

> "I could work as much, and eat as much as a man—when I could get it—and bear the lash as well! And ain't I a woman? I have borne thirteen children and seen most of them sold into slavery, and when I cried out with a mother's grief, none but Jesus heard me. And ain't I a woman?

"He talks about this thing in the head. What's that they call it?"

"Intellect," whispered a woman nearby.

"That's it, honey. What's intellect got to do with women's rights or black folks' rights? If my cup won't hold but a pint and yours holds a quart, wouldn't you be mean not to let me have my little half-measure full?

"That little man in black there! He says women can't have as much rights as men. 'Cause Christ wasn't a woman. Where did your Christ come from?

"Where did your Christ come from? From God and a woman! Man had nothing to do with Him!...If the first woman God ever made was strong enough to turn the world upside down all alone, these women together... ought to be able to turn it back and get it right side up again."[1]

That speech raised the audience to their feet in wild cheers. Why? Because it is great advice. We women *can* team up to turn the world right side up again!

One Ordinary Woman

You might be saying, "But I'm just one ordinary woman." That's just it. We're all ordinary, but our God is extraordinary! On my tombstone I want written, *One ordinary woman impassioned by God CAN make a difference.* And, girls, what a difference we can make! If we stand shoulder to shoulder and link arms, we can be a united front for what is good, right, decent, moral, loving, and just. But we have to *want* to!

When I was a young director of women's ministry, I approached a woman over 50 with, what I thought was, an exciting ministry opportunity. She looked me square in the eye and said, "Honey, I have done my time."

"I have done my time." She said it as though it were a prison sentence rather than a partnership with the living God. I vowed then and there, *Lord, never let me get that "Been there, done that, bought the T-shirt" attitude.* Instead, I want to be more like my grandmother, who was honored for being a "pink lady," a dedicated hospital volunteer, serving almost until the day she died. It was an incredible sight to see. My feeble, frail, thin grandmother would haul her little portable oxygen tank to the nursing home every week to set hair, pass out magazines, distribute snacks, and hand out Kleenex. If she didn't have that pink frock on, people might have mistaken her for a patient.

You Are Needed, Sister!

The world needs us to stay involved and engaged. They need our wisdom, and we need to be the good people who are willing to stand up and make a difference in a broken world. There is a famous poem, penned by a pastor battling Hitler in Nazi Germany:

> *First they came for the Jews*
> *and I did not speak out because I was not a Jew.*
> *Then they came for the Communists*
> *and I did not speak out because I was not a Communist.*
> *Then they came for the trade unionists*
> *and I did not speak out because I was not a trade unionist.*
> *Then they came for me and there was no one left*
> *to speak out for me.*[2]

Check out a few of these statistics that remind each of us that we live in a very fallen world:

- Not very many years ago, a child's first exposure to pornography was typically at age 11. Now it's down to five years of age.[3]

- One out of every six women, including Christians, struggles with an addiction to pornography.[4] Women, far more than men, are likely to act out their behaviors in real life, such as having multiple partners, casual sex, or affairs.[5]

- Each year, more than a million children are exploited in the global commercial sex trade.[6]

- Nonmarital births increased by 242.6 percent between 1970 and 2003.[7] Children raised without a father in the home are more likely to experience emotional and behavioral problems, school failure, drug and alcohol abuse, crime, and incarceration.[8]

- Mothers who have never been married experience domestic violence at more than twice the rate of mothers who have been, or currently are, married.[9]

- Every six minutes a woman is raped.[10]

- More than 15 million new cases of STDs occur every year.[11] Nearly two-thirds of STDs occur in people younger than 25 years of age.[12]

- Survey data from 1999 indicate that 19.3 percent of high school students had seriously considered attempting suicide, 14.5 percent had made plans to attempt suicide, and 8.3 percent had made a suicide attempt during the year preceding the survey.[13] Suicide deaths outnumber homicide deaths by five to three.[14]

- The estimated number of diagnoses of AIDS through 2004 in the United States is 944,305—9,443 of these AIDS cases were estimated in children under age 13.[15] The number of people living with HIV globally is an estimated 40.3 million people. More than 3 million people died of AIDS-related illnesses in 2005; of these, more than 500,000 were children.[16]

- Worldwide, one in three women has been beaten, abused, or coerced into having sex. "According to Amnesty International, this year 200 women in Bangladesh will be burned and disfigured by acid thrown on them as revenge by in-laws and suitors...7000 women a year die in India as a result of dowry disputes...Women are frequently murdered by male family members in some societies for 'dishonoring' their family, such as refusing to marry, suspicion of extramarital affairs, or rape."[17] These are called "honor killings."

- One billion of the 2.2 billion children on the planet live in poverty, often lacking adequate food, shelter, water, and health care.[18]

- More than 250 million Christians around the world are trapped in situations of violence, oppression, and fear—just because they are committed to their faith.[19]

She Did What She Could

Are you completely overwhelmed? Me too, but we cannot allow ourselves to hide because the needs are so big. When I think about the needs of the world, I do what my friend and speaker Marilyn Williams advises. While studying Scripture, she came across this verse, "She did what she could" (Mark 14:8 NIV). We can't do it all, so we do what we can. We sponsor a child for $30 a month. We buy Christmas cards from former prostitutes in a women's shelter in India. We buy Christmas gifts from websites of women helping women in third world countries, or of products made by members of the persecuted church to give other mommies a helping hand out of poverty. We walk for breast cancer. We volunteer a few hours in a crisis pregnancy center or rape crisis center. We offer a phone number or an e-mail address to a woman in pain. We give to missionaries. We use our gifts and talents to team with organizations we believe in. We can't do it all—but we can do *something*. As we keep doing our small part, knitting our piece of the quilt to help humanity, God stitches our hearts and efforts together and creates a blanket of hope for the world. What piece of the quilt of love has God asked *you* to carry?

The editor of *More* magazine says, "The items on my own to-do list have shifted in recent years. Like many of you, I've put giving back closer to the top. It's women over 40 who are driving both volunteerism and philanthropy these days, and in the process, we're revolutionizing both."[20] It's time for a revolution of love.

A Vessel of Love

There is a little garden in Phoenix, Arizona, and another one like it in Darmstadt, Germany, that stands as a tower and powerful reminder of what can be accomplished with "girl power." I went to the garden in Germany when I was asked to speak to the military wives across Europe who were involved with Protestant Women of the Chapel (PWOC). It was the week after their husbands were deployed to Iraq. I stepped off the plane and Debbie, my hostess, took me to this precious garden. Debbie didn't know that I had just experienced my worst day personally and professionally before I stepped on that plane.

Life felt so unjust in my little world. Bill was sick, and people's responses were sometimes hard to understand and even hurtful. I knew I would be coming home to a complete life change because Bill resigned his post the day I left. I got on that plane completely empty and struggling to maintain hope. I felt so unworthy to speak to such an amazing group of courageous women who had kissed their husbands farewell, maybe for the last time, and were coming to this event to be spiritually fed. I needed a spiritual heart transplant!

A friend in Seasoned Sisters had prayed that God would give me a few seats together so I could rest better, and God gave me a whole row! I stretched out, put on my headphones, and listened to the Bible on CD and praise music all the way over. It was 24 hours of the truth turned up loud. By God's grace, I felt encouraged when I landed. Then Debbie took me to this garden, created by the Evangelical Sisterhood of Mary as soon as I got off the plane so I could better adjust to the time change. Its founders, Mother Basilea (Dr. Klara Schlink) and Mother Martyria (Erika Madauss), were single women who stood up against Hitler and his tyranny. When the war ended, Klara felt called by God to gather a group of women to begin a center for love in Germany to redeem the inhumanity Hitler had perpetrated.

She wanted to create a conference center where God's love could be proclaimed to the world. So these precious women, who had no cars, *gathered the bricks in their aprons and walked,* sometimes up to six miles each way, to build the first chapel on the grounds. As I walked through the garden with its beautiful depictions of all Christ had done for us on the cross, I thought of all those women had done and all that Jesus had done to bring love to me. *Lord, how can I give back? How can I be a vessel of Your love and light? These women walked miles, with bricks in their aprons. Such sacrifice! Jesus, You walked up Golgotha's hill with a cross on Your ripped and torn back. Such sacrifice! Dear Lord, what path do You have for me? I want to be a funnel for Your love. Show me the steps, and I will take one obedient step at a time. Please allow me the privilege of walking the path of love's light.*

It's Worth the Wait

Dreams are often deferred, but it may be that very prayer, or hope, you have carried for ages that God will allow to work out in life's second half. My friend Marilyn carried a burden for years for the war-torn nations of Africa, but poor health kept her from going overseas. Then in her fortieth year, God allowed her health to prosper, and she received a letter from the Ivory Coast inviting her to speak at a women's event. Apparently, the daughter of a high government official had heard Marilyn's story at a small MOPS meeting while she was in the States. Marilyn's story of overcoming personal pain through God's power ushered her into a keynote position, and she was asked to speak in the palace before the president! Don't give up the dream!

Change Course

Other times, we receive our mission assignments in the middle of what appears to be a crisis or the loss of a dream. I am convinced

Seasoned Sisters would not have been born in my heart except for the years of personal pain God allowed to come my way. An even better example is that of my friend Carol Kent, an international speaker and author of *When I Lay My Isaac Down*. Carol comes from a strong, loving Christian family. She has a terrific marriage to Gene, and her son was a decorated Naval Academy grad. *Life couldn't get better than this!* she thought, until one day they received a phone call that her only son was arrested on murder charges. Her world went from time spent in churches each week to an entirely different ministry to prisoners and their families through a non-profit organization they established called Speak Up for Hope.

Sometimes our loss is the world's great gain. That is the story of former congresswoman Linda Smith. In an interview with *Today's Christian Woman Magazine,* her life is described:

> "That's a picture of Renu; she's working in one of our safe houses…here's Mannisha, who was a brothel baby, holding her first doll…," she tells me. Linda knows all the names of the women in the photos; she knows the intimate details of their stories, too—tales of abandonment, torture, rape, despair, and then unexpected hope and healing in Christ.
>
> These pictures hang on the walls of Shared Hope International (SHI), the Vancouver, Washington-based nonprofit organization Linda founded in November 1998 to rescue and aid women who have been trafficked as sex slaves. The passion Linda has for SHI is obvious. But it's still a bit surprising to hear the 53-year-old former U.S. Congresswoman from Washington State express joy about the event that helped her launch SHI: losing an election.
>
> "When I ran for the U.S. Senate in 1998, I didn't win— which was God's great plan!" Linda proclaims. In fact, Linda says everything in her life up to this point has been readying her for her role as executive director of Shared Hope International.

Linda launched her political career in 1983 when she defeated an incumbent to become a member of the Washington State Legislature. A doggedly determined pro-life, anti-euthanasia, and campaign-finance-reform advocate who subsequently won several state elections, Linda, her husband, Vern, and her two children often were the target of smear tactics because of her conservative Christian views. Then a remarkable write-in campaign in her home district catapulted Linda into Congress in 1994. Never one to shy from tackling a human-rights issue, Linda was a rare female pro-life voice in Congress, fighting girl infanticide and defending females sold and marketed as commodities to human brokers around the world. Today Linda has become the nation's leading nongovernmental activist in the issue of sex trafficking.

After traveling to Calcutta, where she saw women and children, some as young as her own six-year-old granddaughter in stalls, caged for sex slavery, Linda's passion propelled her to action:

> As soon as I returned home, I founded Shared Hope. Within a month, we (Shared Hope) opened our first "safe house" in Bombay to provide shelter for these girls; before six months were up, we'd opened nine. Today we have the capacity to care for about 500 girls…During my 1998 Senate race, 35,000 people contributed to my campaign. After I lost the election, I sent letters to everyone saying, "We didn't win the U.S. Senate race, but I've started this other organization. This is where I'm going to invest my life." I sent the contributions back, but many people signed them over to Shared Hope. I was able to raise a half million dollars immediately. God prepared me for this opportunity.[21]

What has God spent a lifetime preparing you for?

How Do I Discover My Destiny?

Many a woman at midlife just needs some clarification and permission to pursue the calling or passion that has long been on her heart. I encourage women with, "Take a look back in order to go forward." What are those spiritual road markers God has put in your life to point the way to the next step in your future? As I look back on my life, growing up in the home of a raging dad with drinking problems, I gained a few things:

- A heart for victims of domestic violence.

- A heart for girls who are looking for love in all the wrong places.

- A conviction that all women need mentors because mentors made such a dramatic difference for the better in my life.

- I grew up encouraged by my mom and grandmother to take the lead. Being dance captain, gymnastics' team captain, and even head cheerleader prepared me to be comfortable in a leadership position.

- In elementary school, I won a speech contest and discovered I enjoyed sharing truths from the Bible in a humorous and practical way to impart life change.

Because of God's great mercy and redemptive power, I married well, so teaching others the relationship skills that have made our marriage and family work became a natural next step in giving back. Watching my own mother treated unjustly gave me a heart for any woman in any kind of an unjust situation. As I watched her grow, I became convinced that God values women and longs to entrust them with ministry.

An easy way to begin to discern your destiny is to make a list of five to seven times when you gave your life away, when you were other-centered, and you thought afterward, "That went well" or "I think God used me!" Write out descriptions of these times and then go back and see if there are any repeating patterns. Are there repeating words such as: listen, hospitality, organize, social or political issues? Is there a repeating people group? Women of similar age, children, women in pain, married couple, singles? Are you seeing the repeated use of a certain gift or talent? Music, helps, leadership, spokesperson, writing? Look for the repeating pattern and start serving in that area. Soon you'll see what a difference *you* are making!

Terrific Top Two

There are two very obvious things every woman is called to do. We are called to "go and make disciples of all nations...teaching them to obey" all that Jesus commanded (Matthew 28:19-20 NIV). And we are commissioned to teach younger women (Titus 2:3-5). In other words, we are to mentor and disciple. Younger women long for us to build into their lives—really they do! They want to hear from you—trust me on this!

Some of the young women are single college students who may not have Christian moms. Just open up your heart, home, and relationship with God and invite younger women in to hang out with you. There are a host of books you can use as curriculum. (*Woman of Influence* and *The 10 Best Decisions a Woman Can Make* are two I wrote for this.) Maybe you have a heart for young moms, so groups like MOPS, Hearts at Home, and Moms in Touch all need leaders. Perhaps you can begin a small group in your home and simply answer young moms' questions and help them learn basic life skills like cooking, cleaning, and childrearing.

Maybe you have a desire to be a relationship mentor and help dating or engaged couples, or newlyweds with marriage/relationship learning. Or maybe you gravitate to helping women overcome obstacles like poverty, lack of education, addictions, or cycles of violence or abuse. God gives us lots of elbow room in designing what our mentoring and discipleship looks like. All He asks is that we do it and we do it consistently.

I have always loved mentoring younger women. Sixteen to 26 years of age is my favorite age range because most of life's major decisions are made during these years. Women answer questions such as: Who am I? What are my talents? What's my major? What is my path to education? What is my calling? Will I marry? Whom? Will I have children? When? I find that spending time with these younger women keeps my heart intact. I keep hold of my idealism because they are wide-eyed and excited about life. At a time when we are filled with our own self-doubts, such as "Am I still valued?" younger women will speak the truth to you and will tell you "Thanks" (sometimes when others in your life forget to tell you).

While writing this book, I celebrated Mother's Day out of town with my family. While I was out, one of the young women I mentored called to wish her "spiritual mom" a Happy Mother's Day. Why do I mentor? Because once, a long time ago, I was that young woman at the crossroads and someone took the time to love me. It made a world of difference in my life. Who is the woman, or women, God is calling *you* to tuck under *your* wing and nurture?

Called to Share

We are also clearly commanded to "always be prepared to give an answer to everyone who asks you to give the reason for the hope that you have" (1 Peter 3:15 NIV). We are called to tell others about our best friend, Jesus. My friend Nancy and her husband, Roger, are pastors of a mega church. I believe their church got as big as it is because they know how to love. For example, when they go out to eat, Nancy will simply ask the waitress, "We are getting ready to bless our food and thank God, but we also wanted to know, is there anything we can pray about for you?"

One time the waiter went to get a cook out of the kitchen who needed prayer for her family. Another time the waitress first said, "No, thanks. I don't believe," but then she chased them down later in the parking lot to get prayer when she got news she had cancer. Love always wins out. That doesn't mean we have to agree with all the life choices and every statement a pre-believer makes, but love finds a way. Love is Jesus talking to the woman at the well when no one else would talk to her because they looked down on her. Love is Jesus stopping a stoning of an adulterous woman and pointing out that any in the crowd who is without any sin can throw the first stone. Love is Jesus healing a blind man, a leper, a hemorrhaging woman, instead of blaming them for their poor plight in life. Love takes the higher road and asks, "What is this person's greatest need and what is this person's *presenting* need?" Then love seeks to meet the need. *We give people what they most need wrapped in what they might be willing to listen to.* Love is going just a little out of our way to communicate to someone, "You are valuable. God thinks so. I think so."

Heart Shift Questions

To be willing to care, each of us periodically needs a heart shift. When it is your turn, simply ask these three questions:

1. "Lord, who in my world needs to see You more clearly?" Is it someone who services your life? The manicurist, massage therapist, dog groomer, or the Avon salesperson? Who does your world touch naturally?

2. "Lord, what would You like me to *say* to show love and care for this person?" Usually God will first have you ask a whole lot of questions. Build a bridge of trust and care to their heart.

3. "Lord, what do You want me to do to show Your love to them?" Is it an offer to take her to lunch? To pick up her child from school when she is in a pinch for a sitter? Is it sharing an article, a magazine, a book, a CD or DVD that you found meaningful and now want to give to her? Is it listening to her woes and offering to pray, or to rally help to facilitate a tangible, positive life-change in her world?

Often on airplanes I will walk back to the restroom and, after I take my turn, I hang out in the galley or near it. I do a few simple stretches and ask the flight crew about their world. I often begin the conversation with a compliment. "Wow, I really admire flight attendants. You have to deal with tired people all day, who often are not on their best behavior, and you do it with such graciousness and patience. You are incredible people." (And I mean it!)

Those simple, kind words have opened up so many conversations. I have prayed with flight attendants over their futures, their children, their marriages, and their decisions, and all it ever starts with is a simple "Thank you." You will be surprised by God as you decide to become an ambassador of His love. He will send you to exciting places, and your life will be enriched by the relationships you will make along the way. And it will be an adventure. A young woman I mentor has also served with Youth With A Mission (YWAM). They have a slogan, "Ruined for the normal," which means that once you have tasted a life of faith as an ambassador of love for God, you never want to go back to the status quo.

Adventure with God

This attitude of being on adventure with God is one Lynne Hybels picks up on in her book *Nice Girls Don't Change the World*. Instead of being nice girls who are simply people pleasers, Lynne challenges women to go beyond the status quo to become "good women." Lynne writes, " A good woman...sings her song even if she is terrified. Whatever she is called to do, she does it, evens if she is so scared her voices breaks, her hands shake, and her stomach aches. She doesn't let fear stop her."

Once Lynne, in a midlife crisis of her own, prayed to God, "I don't know how to move into the future. So I am going to pray for your guidance. I am going to listen for your voice. And then I am going to do whatever you tell me to do." And she sensed God saying, "Okay, I will guide you. I will lead you into the future. But if you really want my guidance, you better get ready for an adventure.

You better prepare yourself for new challenges and unexpected opportunities. You better get ready to learn and stretch and grow."

Then Lynne candidly shares, "I've...learned that my first response to just about everything is fear. If I listened to the voice of fear, I would do basically nothing. But part of what it means to move from being a nice girl to a good woman is that I choose to talk down fear. When fear says, 'What have you gotten yourself into now?' I say, 'I think I have gotten myself into the will of God, and I am not going to back down.' "[22] "At the beginning of this book, I said the opposite of a nice girl is a good woman. But what I really wanted to say—and what I am going to say now—is the opposite of a nice girl is not just a good woman, but a downright dangerous woman. A woman who shows up with everything she is and joins the battle against whatever opposes the Word of God in our lives and in our world. A dangerous woman delves deeply into the truth of who she is, grounds herself daily in the healing and empowering love of God, and radically engages the needs of the world...Dangerous women. World-changing women..."[23]

While at the Boston marathon, Lynne saw a woman run by in a T-shirt that captured this heart for adventure. It simply read on the front, "Done watching" and on the back, "Doing!"

My own heart danced for joy as I read those words because years before, after I heard Lynne's message at a Purpose-Driven conference where we were both speaking, I was so overcome by God's power through her words that I said something like, "Lynne, that was anointed! You have got to write your story. Your life will encourage and inspire millions of women."

Are you ready for the adventure of a lifetime?

Stay Replenished

If you are going to stay on the front lines of being a world-changer and difference-maker in life's second half, you have to take care of your energy level. One way I have discovered, other than the obvious means of exercising, eating right and sleeping enough, is to have a "balancer," or something that I love to do that renews me. For you, this could be anything: ballroom or square dancing with your spouse, bike riding or kayaking with girlfriends, going back to school and keeping your mind renewed and growing, time with grandchildren just playing, travel, launching a company, or writing a book.

We are at life's pinnacle, a defining point, much like the evaluation we had in our early twenties or thirties when we asked, Who am I, God? At this crossroads, as our children leave home and we find expendable time, we ask, With the remaining years, what can I do that will really matter? What will leave a lasting legacy? We are on a search for significance.

In our support group, some of the most challenging questions we have discussed are: What have you always wanted to do but were too afraid or too busy to do until now? What is a great adventure you'd like to do before your body wears out? What is a dream yet unfulfilled? What is a goal God has yet to accomplish?

My friend Lori was out on a date with her husband, to whom she had been married for more than 20 years. Out of the blue he asked, "Honey, what are your dreams for the future?" Lori gave what might be a list of normal expected dreams: the kids will marry, we'll have grandchildren, we'll retire, etc. But then he asked, "No, what are your personal, secret, longed for dreams?"

She thought long about this unexpected question and then answered, "I have always wanted to ice skate."

Months went by, and Lori thought little about the isolated question from their date night. That is until Christmas morning, when a big square box was tucked under the tree with her name on it. It was heavy when she picked it up. As she unfolded the tissue, two beautiful new ice skates appeared with a gift certificate for lessons. Today, Lori is training for her first "master's" (over 40) skate competition and her husband, Mike, plans to be her fan, sitting front and center rink side.

Maybe you have allowed a dream to get set aside because of the needs of your family. When Sheryl was in her early forties with two children in college, she recaptured a skill she had let go dormant—flying airplanes! As a young woman, she learned to fly but family responsibilities forced her to set aside her love. As she has stepped out to capture this love, she has discovered a new career as well. She is becoming a flight instructor! When we had breakfast recently, I noticed a large pile of very thick manuals and books on her back-seat—all flight manuals. We both bemoaned that learning and memorizing is much more difficult in life's second half, but to Sheryl the price is worth it. Her eyes danced and her smile bright-ened as she talked of soaring into the wild blue yonder. Are you ready to soar?

What are your "must do before I die" things? A few of mine are: *A master's swim race; maybe a triathlon; biking through Europe or the back roads of America; kayaking some of America's best bays and rivers; travel to the military bases worldwide to minister to troops and their families; write a novel; help young people recapture the real meaning of love and romance so they can experience the kind of happy marriage I have known; learn to ballroom dance; go to the places of my family history: England, Germany, the Trails of Tears; spend two weeks alone on a secluded island with my husband; help my kids fix up their homes; run a cousins' camp (like a vacation Bible School) for my grandkids (when they arrive someday!); build a cabin for our extended family and friends to use for rest and for ministry; travel the world to equip and encourage Christian leaders and pastors; travel to the Holy Land; plan and host an international Seasoned Sisters conference where we'd have a whole lot of fun!* I am not sure if God will allow me the time, energy, or money to do everything on the list, but I do know that having the list gives me something to look forward to. There is light at the end of the responsibility tunnel.

Woman of Action

Sometimes people tell me, "Pam, you are so intense." As though intensity is a bad thing. When I read Proverbs 31 about the woman who is held up as a role model (almost every Mother's Day in sermons), well, she seems a bit "intense" too. When I was studying the passage for myself, I saw a pattern in the text that encouraged me. Proverbs 31:12-27 contains a poem explaining a woman of noble character. I have italicized some of the verbs in the passage:

- She *brings* him good, not harm, all the days of her life.

- She *selects* wool and flax and *works* with eager hands.

- She is like the merchant ships, *bringing* her food from afar.

- She *gets up* while it is still dark; she *provides* food for her family and portions for her servant girls.

- She *considers* a field and *buys* it; out of her earnings she *plants* a vineyard.

- She *sets* about her work vigorously; her arms are strong for her tasks.

- She *sees* that her trading is profitable, and her lamp *does not go out* at night.

- In her hand she *holds* the distaff and *grasps* the spindle with her fingers.

- She *opens* her arms to the poor and *extends* her hands to the needy.

- She *makes* coverings for her bed; she *is clothed* in fine linen and purple.

- She *makes* linen garments and *sells* them, and *supplies* the merchants with sashes.

- She is clothed with strength and dignity; she *can laugh* at the days to come.

- She *speaks* with wisdom, and faithful instruction is on her tongue.

- She *watches* over the affairs of her household and does not eat the bread of idleness.

Do you see a common thread? She's in action! What is the result of this "press into the tape at the finish line" attitude?

> Her children rise up and bless her; her husband also, and he praises her, saying: "Many daughters have done nobly, but you excel them all." Charm is deceitful and beauty is vain, but a woman who fears the LORD, she shall be praised. Give her the product of her hands, and let her works praise her in the gates (Proverbs 31:28-31).

Are you getting this down, girl? Our kin will be praising us at the city gates, which, in our culture, would be the equivalent to something like, "They will be shouting your praise on *Oprah!*" All because we became women who feared the Lord and let that awe move us to action. Notice the last line: "Give her the product of her hands and let her works praise her in the gates." The predictable consequences of your life of action, the dominos of good deeds, the centripetal force of your caring heart is a party "at the gates" in honor of *you* and all GOD has done *through you!* Take action—get a little "dangerous" for God—and let the party begin!

— *Joy Choice* —

To me, joy is leaving the world better than you found it and introducing as many people as possible to the Savior.

As you read through this chapter, which statistics or stories either made you weepy or angry? Tap into those emotions to signal the cause that God may be calling you to. What is at least one key issue you will carry a mantle for in the second half of life?

How are you staying informed? Connect yourself to a group like Concerned Women for America, Focus on the Family, American Family Association, or Masterful Living (our organization). I receive e-zines from these groups and then I take five minutes to do something: make a call, write an e-mail, etc. Your five minutes could impact someone else's lifetime.

You are a mentor, a discipler, a woman of wisdom that young women would love to spend time with. Who is the one (or more than one) young woman you will invest time in during this next year?

Because you are a caring, compassionate woman, God will keep you on the battlefield. He will find a place for you to serve Him to make this world a little better place and to help people gain a personal relationship with Him. Every good soldier, however, needs some R and R to keep them battle ready. What is the one fun balancer you will do to stay replenished?

Notes

Chapter 1—The Rest Can Be the Best!

Epigraph: <www.chy.com.au/seminars.htm>.
1. Nancy Gibbs, "Bring It On," *Time* magazine, May 16, 2005, p. 54.
2. <www.marketingprofs.com/login/signup.asp?source=/5/brown1.asp>.
3. Verse by Susan Malachowski, Leanin' Tree, Boulder, CO. Used by permission.
4. David Jeremiah, *A Bend in the Road: Finding God When Your World Caves In* (Nashville, TN: W Publishing Group, 2002), p. 18.

Chapter 2—You Gotta Have Friends

Epigraph: Leigh Anne Jasheway-Bryant.
1. The use of private e-mails throughout this book is by permission of all parties.
2. Psalm 5:12 and Psalm 90:17 NIV.
3. Jill Briscoe, in a message to pastors' wives and leaders, San Marcos, CA, 2002. Quote used by permission.
4. Daisy Hepburn, Pine Valley Women's Retreat, 2002.
5. Author unknown.

Chapter 3—Learning to THRIVE

Epigraph: Ada Lum
1. Gina Kemp, Monika White, and Robert Segal, "Aging Well: A Lesson from Centenarians" from Helpguide, <www.helpguide.org/lifelong_wellness.htm>.
2. Ibid.
3. <ohhowilovejesus.com/2006/04/08/there-is-no-pit-so-deep-that-he-is-not-deeper-still/>.
4. <bible.crosswalk.com/Lexicons/Hebrew/heb.cgi?number=05564&version=>.

5. Personal e-mail from Karen to Pam, June 2006.

6. Personal e-mail from Connie to Pam, June 2006. Check out Connie's website at <www.songsthatpray.com>.

7. <www.buzzle.com/editorials/5-13-2002-18338.asp>.

8. Ibid.

Chapter 4—Get Moving

Epigraph: Joseph Pilates.

1. Author unknown.

2. <www.mayoclinic.com>.

3. Larrian Gillespie, *The Menopause Diet* (Beverly Hills, CA: Healthy Life, 2003), p. xiii.

4. Ibid., p. 199.

5. <www.stressinstitute.com/Resources/WellnessAndSelfCare.aspx>.

6. <seniorliving.about.com/od/retirement/a/newboomerretire.htm>.

7. Jospeh H. Pilates, <www.pilatesmethodalliance.org/whatis.html>.

8. Ibid.

9. Ibid.

10. <www.ynhh.org/healthlink/womens/womens_7_02.html>.

11. <www.praisemoves.com>.

12. <womenshealth.about.com/cs/exercise/a/fitnessplantips.htm>.

13. Marcia Jones and Theresa Eichenwald, *Menopause for Dummies* (New York, NY: Wiley Publishing, 2003), p. 259.

14. Ibid.

Chapter 5—Check Up On Yourself

Epigraph: German proverb.

1. <www.womhealth.org.au/factsheets/aboutmenopause.htm>.

2. <www.buzzle.com/editorials/5-13-2002-18338.asp>.

3. Marcia Jones and Theresa Eichenwald, *Menopause for Dummies* (New York, NY: Wiley Publishing, 2003), p. 137.

4. Colette Bouchez, *Your Perfectly Pampered Menopause* (New York, NY: Broadway Books, 2005), p. 298.

5. Larrian Gillespie, *The Menopause Diet* (Beverly Hills, CA: Healthy Life, 2003), p. 112.

6. Angela Stengler and Mark Stengler, *Your Menopause, Your Menotype* (New York, NY: Penguin Group, Inc., 2003), p. xvii.

7. Ibid., p. 4.

8. <www.breastcancer.org/dia_detec_exam_5step.html>.

9. This piece was the 2003 winner of the Erma Bombeck humor competition. Written by Leigh Anne Jasheway-Bryant of Eugene, Oregon, <ww.accidental comic.com>. Used by permission.

10. <womenshealth.about.com/cs/abnormalbleeding/a/abnuterbleeding.htm>.

11. <womenshealth.about.com/od/abnormalbleeding/a/causemenorrhagi.htm>.

12. <www.womenshealth.gov/faq/hysterectomy.htm>.

13. Ibid.

14. Ibid.

Chapter 6—Longer and Stronger

Epigraph: Danna Demetre.

1. "Aging Gracefully," copyright © 2002 by Maria Rote. All rights reserved. Used by permission.

2. Marcia Jones and Theresa Eichenwald, *Menopause for Dummies* (New York, NY: Wiley Publishing, 2003), p. 259.

3. Colette Bouchez, *Your Perfectly Pampered Menopause* (New York, NY: Broadway Books, 2005), p. 185.

4. Larrian Gillespie, *The Menopause Diet* (Beverly Hills, CA: Healthy Life, 2003), p. 9.

5. Ibid., preface.

6. Ibid., pp. 2-3.

7. <www.mendosa.com/gilists.htm>.

8. Laurette Willis, *BASIC Steps to Godly Fitness* (Eugene, OR: Harvest House Publishers, 2005), p. 33.

9. Personal e-mail to Pam, June 2006.

10. <www.rediff.com/getahead/2004/dec/08sleep.htm>.

11. Ibid.

12. Colette Bouchez, *Your Perfectly Pampered Menopause* (New York, NY: Broadway Books, 2005), p. 189.

13. <www.nhlbi.nih.gov/new/press/05-02-04.htm>.

14. <www.canadian-health-network.ca/servlet/ContentServer?cid=1001992&page name=CHN-RCS%2FCHNResource%2FFAQCHNResourceTemplate&c=CH NResource&lang=En>.

15. <www.project-aware.org/Managing/exercise.shtml>.

16. <www.nhlbi.nih.gov/hbp/prevent/sodium/sodium.htm>.

17. <www.womhealth.org.au/factsheets/aboutmenopause.htm>. Normal bone density

is when the T score measures between 0 and -1; Osteopaenia is diagnosed when T scores are between -1 and -2.5. Osteopaenia is when there is some bone loss, but it's not severe enough to be called osteoporosis; Osteoporosis is diagnosed when the T score measures -2.5 or less.

18. Marcia Jones and Theresa Eichenwald, *Menopause for Dummies* (New York, NY: Wiley Publishing, 2003), p. 259.

19. <www.asbs.org/html/bmi.html?site_id=1&page_id=25>.

20. To order *Scale Down* or Caltrac, go to <www.dannademetre.com>.

21. To find a physician who will give these extra kinds of tests and provide treatment that may include more natural forms of science, nutrition, and supplements, call the American Association of Naturopathic Physicians at 866-538-2267 or go to <www.naturopathic.org>.

22. <www.more.com/more/printableStory.jsp?catref=cat5320008&storyid=/tem platedata/more/story/data/1150298826315.xml>.

23. William K. Klingman, *Turning 40: Wit, Wisdom and Whining* (New York, NY: Plume, 1992).

Chapter 7—Love Lavishly

Epigraph: 1 Corinthians 13:13.

1. <pewresearch.org/obdeck/?ObDeckID=1>.

2. <www.unmarriedamerica.org/usaweek/factsonsingles.htm>.

3. "A Spinster's Lament," copyright © 1990 by Peggy Rentz. All rights reserved. Used by permission.

4. <www.aarpmagazine.org/family/Articles/a2004-05-26-mag-divorce.html>.

5. Dear Abby, PO Box 69440, Los Angeles, CA 90069.

6. Author unknown.

7. E-mail, April 2006, used by permission.

Chapter 8—It's All Relatively CALM

Epigraph: Saying from a magnet on Pam's refrigerator.

1. Larrian Gillespie, *The Menopause Diet* (Beverly Hills, CA: Healthy Life, 2003), p. x.

2. Sarah Groves, *Station Wagon*, "Small Piece of You," © 2004 Sara Groves Music (admin. by Music Services). All Rights Reserved. ASCAP. Used by permission.

3. Elyse Fitzpatrick, *The Afternoon of Life* (Phillipsburg, NJ: P&R Publishing, 2004), p. 84.

Chapter 9—Calming the Chaos

Epigraph: Bill Dodds, *How to Survive Your 40th Birthday* (Minnetonka, MN: Meadowbrook Press, 1990), p. 41.

1. This concept appears in several of our books: *Love, Honor and Forgive* (IVP), *Men Are Like Waffles—Women Are Like Spaghetti* (Harvest House), and in DVD format by Lifeway.
2. Leigh Anne Jasheway, *I'm Not Getting Older (I'm Getting Better at Denial)* (Eugene, OR: The Comedy Workout, 1999).

Chapter 10—Monitor Your Money

Epigraph: Author unknown.

1. For financial insights from Ellie, please check out her website at <www.elliekay. com>. Material used herein by permission.
2. <www.cbsnews.com/stories/2006/03/22/eveningnews/main1431707.shtml>.
3. <blogs.usatoday.com/ondeadline/2006/04/arthur_winston_.html>.
4. <www.apta.com/passenger_transport/thisweek/060424_3.cfm>.
5. Humberto Cruz, "Dreamers, You Need to Wake Up," *Kansas City Star,* April 30, 2006, News, H8.
6. <www.news.harvard.edu/gazette/1998/10.01/WhyWomenLiveLon.html>.
7. <www.forbes.com/finance/2006/04/28/marriage-financial-planning-cx_sr_0501marriageseven.html>.
8. Humberto Cruz, "Dreamers, You Need to Wake Up," *Kansas City Star,* April 30, 2006. News, H8.
9. Ibid.
10. Ibid.
11. <www.lsuagcenter.com/en/money_business/personal_finance/money_manage ment/Strategies+for+Successful+Retirement.htm>.

Chapter 11—New Horizons

Epigraph: Eleanor Roosevelt.

1. <afgen.com/sojourner1.html>.
2. Pastor Martin Niemöller, <www.telisphere.com/~cearley/sean/camps/first. html>.
3. Frank York and Jan LaRue, *Protecting Your Child in an X-Rated World* (Colorado Springs, CO: Focus on the Family Publishing, 2002), p. 12.
4. <www.christianitytoday.com/tcw/2003/005/5.58.html>.
5. Ibid.

6. <www.state.gov/g/tip/rls/tiprpt/2005/46606.htm>.

7. <www.cwfa.org/articledisplay.asp?id=8761&department=BLI&categoryid=family>.

8. <www.heritage.org/Research/Welfare/tst021005a.cfm>.

9. From the 1999 National Crime Victimization Survey as quoted by Patrick F. Fagan and Kirk A. Johnson, in "Marriage: The Safest Place for Women and Children," Heritage Foundation Backgrounder No. 1535, April 10, 2002.

10. Pam Farrel, *The 10 Best Decisions a Woman Can Make* (Eugene, OR: Harvest House Publishers, 2004), p. 137.

11. <www.guttmacher.org/pubs/tgr/05/3/gr050308.html>.

12. <www.cwfa.org/images/content/kuala-lumpur.pdf.>

13. "Youth Risk Behavior Surveillance—United States, 1999. In: CDC Surveillance Summaries, June 9, 2000. *MMWR* 2000, p. 10.

14. E.K. Moscicke, "Epidemiology of Completed and Attempted Suicide: Toward a Framework for Prevention," *Clinical Neuroscience Research,* 2001; 1:310-23.

15. <www.cdc.gov/hiv/topics/surveillance/basic.htm>.

16. <www.unaids.org/epi/2005/doc/docs/PR_EpiUpdate_Nov05_en.pdf>.

17. <www.globalgrassroots.org/womens_issues.htm>.

18. <www.compassion.com/about/press/currentnews/compassionsunday.htm>.

19. <www.csw.org.uk/TakeAction/SignUp.htm>.

20. Editor Peggy Northrop of *More* magazine, May 2006.

21. <www.christianitytoday.com/tcw/2004/001/1.30.html>. For more information on Shared Hope International, write to PO Box 65337, Vancouver, WA 98665, call 1-866-HER-LIFE, or check out <www.sharedhope.org>.

22. Lynne Hybels, *Nice Girls Don't Change the World* (Grand Rapids, MI: Zondervan, 2005), pp. 75-76.

23. Ibid., pp. 89-91.

About the Author

Pam Farrel is the cofounder and codirector, along with her husband, Bill, of Masterful Living, an organization that provides practical insights for personal relationships. Pam is also the author of several books to encourage women: *The 10 Best Decisions a Woman Can Make, Devotions for Women on the Go!* and *Woman of Influence.* Together, Pam and Bill are also regular relationship columnists, and their insights can be found in newspapers in several cities in the United States and Canada, *Just Between Us* magazine, and Crosswalk. com. Their books include *Men Are Like Waffles—Women Are Like Spaghetti; Every Marriage Is a Fixer-Upper; Red-Hot Monogamy; The 10 Best Decisions Every Parent Can Make;* and *Love, Honor and Forgive.* They have been married more than 25 years and have three children and a daughter-in-law.

You may contact Pam by mail at:

Harvest House Publishers
990 Owen Loop North
Eugene, OR 97402

Masterful Living
PO Box 1507
San Marcos, CA 92079
(800) 810-4449

Or through her website: www. farrelcommunications.com

For more information on Seasoned Sisters, small-group discussion questions for this book, or information on resources and wisdom for all of you *Fantastic After 40!* women, go to SeasonedSisters.com (www. seasonedsisters.com).

Other Books
by Pam Farrel

MEN ARE LIKE WAFFLES—WOMEN ARE LIKE SPAGHETTI
Pam and Bill Farrel

Pam and Bill Farrel have created a unique and fun look at how God made us and the many different ways men and women regard life, marriage, and relationships. A must-have for every waffle-and-spaghetti couple.

SINGLE MEN ARE LIKE WAFFLES,
SINGLE WOMEN ARE LIKE SPAGHETTI
Pam and Bill Farrel

This is a fun and positive spin-off from their bestseller written with the single person in mind and includes tools you will find helpful.

RED-HOT MONOGAMY
Pam and Bill Farrel

With their trademark insight, humor, and candid personal perspectives, Pam and Bill reveal the truths about the sexual relationship in marriage and what you need to know to keep the embers burning.

THE 10 BEST DECISIONS EVERY PARENT CAN MAKE
Pam and Bill Farrel

With biblical insight and personal experience, the Farrels encourage you to make the important decisions that will nurture and celebrate your children.

THE 10 BEST DECISIONS A WOMAN CAN MAKE
Pam Farrel

Bestselling author Pam Farrel encourages and equips you to discover your unique place in God's plan.

GOT TEENS?
Jill Savage and Pam Farrel

Jill Savage and Pam Farrel offer commonsense solutions, insightful research, and creative ideas to help you guide your children successfully into adulthood.

HARVEST HOUSE
PUBLISHERS

Other Good
Harvest House Reading

10-MINUTE TIME OUTS FOR BUSY WOMEN
Grace Fox

Grace Fox encourages you to make time for what matters most—your relationship with God. Her real-life stories and Scripture-based prayers will help you understand God's truth and apply it to everyday life.

GETTIN' OLD AIN'T FOR WIMPS
Karen O'Connor

With humor and wisdom, speaker and author Karen O'Connor urges fellow baby boomers to celebrate every moment. Personal and gathered stories capture the trials and joys faced when one survives and surpasses middle-age.

MOTHERHOOD: THE GUILT THAT KEEPS ON GIVING
Julie Ann Barnhill

Bestselling author of *She's Gonna Blow* Julie Ann Barnhill explores how you can overcome the legacy of guilt, celebrate your strengths, trust God's plan for you and your children, and experience the lasting joys of motherhood.

WHAT HAPPENS WHEN WOMEN SAY YES TO GOD
Lysa TerKeurst

In *What Happens When Women Say Yes to God,* (a rerelease of *Radically Obedient, Radically Blessed* with a new cover and updated material), Lysa TerKeurst shares inspiring stories from her own life along with compelling biblical insights as she describes the deep joy and great purpose of a life that honors God.

THE POWER OF A PRAYING® WOMAN
Stormie Omartian

Bestselling author Stormie Omartian's deep knowledge of Scripture and examples from her own life provide guidance for those who seek to trust God, maintain a right heart, and give their lives over to God's purpose.

HARVEST HOUSE
PUBLISHERS